The American Heritage®
Essential Student
Thesaurus

Third Edition

Houghton Mifflin Harcourt
Boston • New York

Editorial and Production Staff

Bruce Nichols, Senior Vice President, Publisher, Adult Trade and Reference

Joseph P. Pickett
Vice President, Executive Editor

Christopher Leonesio
Vice President, Managing Editor

Steven R. Kleinedler
Supervising Editor, Project Editor

Christopher Granniss
Database Production Supervisor

Catherine Pratt
Editor

Sarah Iani
Editorial & Production Coordinator

Peter Chipman
Elizabeth Kassab
Associate Editors

Joyce C. Weston
Text Design

Visit our websites: www.ahdictionary.com or www.hmhbooks.com

ISBN-13: 978-0-547-38564-8

Library of Congress Cataloging-in-Publication Data
The American Heritage essential student thesaurus. -- 3rd ed.
    p. cm.
  Includes index.
  ISBN 978-0-547-38564-8
  1. English language--Synonyms and antonyms. [1. English language--Synonyms and antonyms.] I. Houghton Mifflin Harcourt Publishing Company.
II. Title: Essential student thesaurus.
  PE1591.A53 2010
  423'.1--dc22

                                                            2010019037

Manufactured in the United States of America

1 2 3 4 5 6 7 8 9 10-EB-16 15 14 13 12 11 10

Introduction

Why use a thesaurus?

A thesaurus is a book that lists synonyms and antonyms. Synonyms are words that share the same or nearly the same meaning. Antonyms are words that have opposite or nearly opposite meanings.

Understanding how to use synonyms and antonyms is one of the secrets of good writing. Let's imagine you're writing to some friends far away who have never seen snow. You want to describe a really harsh winter, so you begin:

> *Of course, winter is normally a* **cold** *time of year, but last January was unbelievably* **cold***. The river froze, but the* **cold** *air made skating unbearable! I couldn't wait for spring to arrive so the* **cold** *weather would end.*

You realize something seems wrong. Your words just don't communicate the idea you want to get across, and your friends aren't going to think they've been missing much. How can you make the story sound more exciting? You decide to try your new book, *The American Heritage Essential Student Thesaurus,* and see if it can help. You look up the adjective *cold* and read this note:

cold   **cold, arctic, chilly, cool, frigid, frosty, gelid, glacial, icy**
These adjectives mean marked by a low or an extremely low temperature: *cold* air; an *arctic* climate; a *chilly* day; *cool* water; a *frigid* room; a *frosty* morning; *gelid* seas; *glacial* winds; *icy* hands.
Antonym: hot

Maybe you can improve your description after all, simply by changing a few words:

> *Of course, winter is normally a* **chilly** *time of year, but last January was truly* **frigid***. The river froze, but the* **glacial** *winds made skating unbearable! I couldn't wait for spring to arrive so the* **cold** *weather would end.*

There is nothing wrong with the word *cold*, but if you repeat any word too many times in the same paragraph your writing will sound flat and boring, even if you're telling an exciting story. Choosing among different words with similar meanings also helps you express precisely what you want to say. Suppose you continue this way:

*As soon as the weather warms up, the icicles fall and **break**. You can hear the ice **break** too as the river starts flowing again.*

You feel that these sentences could be improved as well. First of all, you would rather not repeat the word *break*. You would rather use language that better describes the different sights and sounds of breaking icicles and ice. You look up the verb *break* in *The American Heritage Essential Student Thesaurus* and read this note:

break   **break, crack, fracture, burst, splinter, shatter, smash**

These verbs mean to separate or cause to separate into parts or pieces, either by the sudden application of force or by the pressure of internal stress. **Break** is the most general: *That delicate ornament will **break** easily. The window was **broken** by vandals. The bag held so many heavy things that it **broke**.* To **crack** is to break without dividing into parts: *The building's foundation **cracked** during the earthquake. By bumping against the counter I **cracked** the coffeepot, but it didn't leak.* **Fracture** applies to a break or crack in a rigid body: *Heat and pressure caused the bedrock to **fracture**. She **fractured** her hip in the accident.* **Burst** implies a sudden coming apart, especially from internal pressure: *The pipe **burst** during the cold snap. The child **burst** the balloon with a pin.* **Splinter** implies splitting into long, thin, sharp pieces: *The boat's hull **splintered** when it hit the reef. The crowbar **splintered** the jamb, and the door opened.* To **shatter** is to break into many scattered pieces: *The icicle **shattered** when it landed on the front steps. The ball **shattered** the window upon impact.* **Smash** stresses force of blow or impact and suggests complete destruction: *I dropped the vase, and it **smashed** into pieces. The storm winds **smashed** the orchard trees, ruining the harvest.*

You realize how easy it is to rewrite the sentences, making them more accurate, descriptive, and interesting:

*As soon as the weather warms up, the icicles fall and **shatter**. You can hear the ice **crack** too as the river starts flowing again.*

By now you can see that *The American Heritage Essential Student Thesaurus* includes two different types of entries. One type of entry lists words that share a general meaning but do not all mean exactly the same thing. A separate definition is given for each of the words to explain how they vary from the shared definition. *Break* is an example of this type of entry. Another example is the adjective *cry*. Additionally, you will find that at many entries, like *cry*, there are quotations from classic and modern authors and journalists that show you how famous writers have used these words in context:

cry cry, weep, wail, bawl, keen, sob, blubber

These verbs mean to express strong emotion, such as grief, misery, or pain, by shedding tears or making inarticulate sounds. *Cry* and *weep* both involve the shedding of tears: "*She **cried** without trying to suppress any of the noisier manifestations of grief and confusion*" (J. D. Salinger); "*I **weep** for what I'm like when I'm alone*" (Theodore Roethke). *Wail* and *bawl* refer to loud sustained utterance, as in grief, misery, or fear: "*The women . . . began to **wail** together; they mourned with shrill cries*" (Joseph Conrad); "*Her voice was always hoarse. Her Dad said this was because she had **bawled** so much when she was a baby*" (Carson McCullers). *Keen* refers more specifically to wailing and lamentation for the dead: "*It is the wild Irish women **keening** over their dead*" (George A. Lawrence). *Sob* describes weeping or a mixture of broken speech and weeping marked by convulsive breathing or gasping: "***sobbing** and crying, and wringing her hands as if her heart would break*" (Laurence Sterne). *Blubber* refers to noisy shedding of tears accompanied by broken or inarticulate speech: "*When he drew out what had been a fiddle, crushed to morsels in the greatcoat, he **blubbered** aloud*" (Emily Brontë).

The other type of entry lists words that all mean close to the same thing. *Cold* is an example of this type of entry. Another example is the noun *celebrity*:

celebrity celebrity, hero, luminary, name, notable, personage

These nouns refer to a widely known person: *a social **celebrity**; the **heroes** of science; a theatrical **luminary**; a big **name** in sports; a **notable** of the concert stage; a **personage** in the field of philosophy.*

Every word in every entry includes a sample sentence, phrase, or quotation, printed in *italics*, to give you a model of how that word can be used.

If you can't find the word you're looking for, try the index at the back of this book. The index lists all of the words included in the entries. If you looked up *fury*, for example, you would learn that *fury* is one of the synonyms in the note at the word *anger*.

This third edition of *The American Heritage Essential Student Thesaurus* has been completely revised and greatly expanded to provide you with even more word choices. We hope you have fun using it to express yourself with imagination!

accompany   accompany, conduct, escort, chaperone

These verbs mean to be with or to go with another or others. ***Accompany*** suggests going with another on an equal basis: *"One day* [my wife] ***accompanied*** *me, upon some household errand, into the cellar of the old building which our poverty compelled us to inhabit"* (Edgar Allan Poe). ***Conduct*** implies guidance of others: *"A servant* ***conducted*** *me to my bedroom"* (Charlotte Brontë). ***Escort*** stresses protective guidance or official action: *"At every county town a long cavalcade of the principal gentlemen . . .* ***escorted*** *the mayor to the market cross"* (Thomas Macaulay). ***Chaperone*** specifies adult supervision of young persons: *My mother helped* ***chaperone*** *the prom.*

acknowledge   acknowledge, admit, own, confess, concede

These verbs express an acceptance of the reality or truth of something, especially something inconvenient, embarrassing, or detrimental to oneself. To ***acknowledge*** is to openly accept the truth of something that is usually already known or suspected: *She* ***acknowledged*** *her mistake in a statement to the press.* ***Admit*** can suggest the acknowledgment of behavior or intentions that one knows to be wrong, embarrassing, or unseemly: *He* ***admitted*** *under questioning that he had falsified his resumé.* ***Own*** or more commonly ***own up*** stresses acceptance of personal responsibility: *"Recovering addicts . . . say that when you are really in recovery, you want to* ***own up*** *to everything related to your drug use"* (Michael Bamberger). ***Confess*** often suggests disclosure of something that one is uncomfortable keeping to oneself: *I have to* ***confess*** *that I lied to you.* To ***concede*** is to accept, often with reluctance or qualifications, what can not reasonably be denied: *"In the face of incontrovertible findings by the scientific community, the industry then* ***conceded*** *that climate change is happening but is so inconsequential as to be negligible"* (Ross Gelbspan).

active   active, busy, energetic, vigorous, dynamic, lively

These adjectives mean having or displaying energy. ***Active*** is the most general, connoting physical or mental exertion in a variety of contexts: *an* ***active*** *toddler; an* ***active*** *imagination; remained* ***active*** *in later years by walking and swimming.* ***Busy*** suggests engagement in sustained activity on a particular task or job: *a* ***busy*** *newspaper staff rushing to meet the deadline.* ***Energetic*** and ***vigorous*** emphasize performance of an activity or pursuit with enthusiasm or intensity: *an* ***energetic*** *competitor; a* ***vigorous*** *crusader against drunk driving.* ***Dynamic*** connotes energy and forcefulness that often inspire others or bring about change: *a* ***dynamic*** *leader who revitalized the party.* ***Lively*** suggests animated activity or alertness: *a* ***lively*** *folk dance; a* ***lively*** *interest in politics.*

adapt   adapt, accommodate, adjust, conform, fit

These verbs mean to make suitable to or consistent with a particular situation or use: ***adapted*** *themselves to city life; can't* ***accommodate*** *myself to the new*

requirements; **adjusting** *their behavior to the rules;* **conforming** *my life to accord with my moral principles;* **fitting** *the punishment to the crime.*

admonish admonish, reprove, rebuke, reprimand, reproach

These verbs mean to correct or caution critically. **Admonish** implies the giving of advice or a warning in order to rectify or avoid something: *"A gallows erected on an eminence* **admonished** *the offenders of the fate that awaited them"* (William Hickling Prescott). **Reprove** usually suggests a measured disapproval ranging from mild to emphatic: *With a stern look, the teacher* **reproved** *the child for whispering in class.* **Rebuke** and **reprimand** both refer to sharp, often angry criticism from a higher authority: *"Some of the most heated criticism . . . has come from the Justice Department, which rarely* **rebukes** *other agencies in public"* (Howard Kurtz); *"A [university] committee . . . asked its president to* **reprimand** *a scientist who tested gene-altered bacteria on trees"* (New York Times). **Reproach** refers to criticism, sometimes from oneself, arising from a sense of personal disappointment or moral disapproval: *"He bitterly regretted his foolishness, and* **reproached** *himself for weakness of will"* (J.R.R. Tolkien); *"She never* **reproached** *him for his bullying manners at parties"* (Louis Auchincloss).

adventurous adventurous, adventuresome, audacious, daredevil, daring, venturesome

These adjectives mean inclined to undertake risks: **adventurous** *pioneers; an* **adventuresome** *prospector; an* **audacious** *explorer; a* **daredevil** *test pilot;* **daring** *acrobats; a* **venturesome** *investor.*

affectation affectation, pose, air, mannerism

These nouns refer to personal behavior assumed for effect. An **affectation** is an artificial manner or behavior adopted to impress others or call attention to oneself: *"Post-Renaissance scholars often adopted the* **affectation** *of recasting their names in classical form"* (Steven Jay Gould). A **pose** is a false manner or attitude usually intended to win favor or cover up a shortcoming: *His humility is only a* **pose**. **Air,** meaning a distinctive but intangible quality, does not always imply sham: *The director had an* **air** *of authority.* In the plural, however, it suggests affectation and self-importance: *The movie star was putting on* **airs**. **Mannerism** denotes an idiosyncratic trait or quirk that others may find attractive but is often perceived as needlessly distracting: *"I can picture . . . her shaking her hands in that odd* **mannerism,** *like someone wanting to strangle a chicken"* (Jill Dawson).

agitate agitate, churn, convulse, rock, shake

These verbs mean to cause to move to and fro violently: *surface water* **agitated** *by the boat's propeller; a storm* **churning** *the waves; buildings* **convulsed** *by an explosion; a hurricane* **rocking** *trees and houses; an earthquake that* **shook** *the ground.*

agreement   agreement, bargain, compact, covenant, deal, pact

These nouns denote an understanding between parties specifying what is expected of each: *made an **agreement** that I would replace any of the items I lost or damaged; kept my end of the **bargain** and mowed the lawn; made a **compact** to correspond regularly; vows that constituted a **covenant** between the marriage partners; made a **deal** that if her parents got a new dog, she would walk it; a solemn **pact** to support each other in times of trouble.*

aim   aim, direct, level, point, train

These verbs mean to turn something toward an intended goal or target: ***aimed** the camera at the guests; **directed** our attention toward the screen; **leveled** criticism at the administration; **pointing** a finger at the suspect; **trained** the gun on the intruder.*

alone   alone, lonely, lonesome, solitary

These adjectives describe lack of companionship. ***Alone*** emphasizes being apart from others but does not necessarily imply unhappiness: *"The first lesson reading teaches is how to be **alone**"* (Jonathan Franzen). ***Lonely*** and ***lonesome*** usually connote painful awareness of being alone: *"'No doubt they are dead,' she thought, and felt . . . sadder and . . . **lonelier** for the thought"* (Ouida); *"You must keep up your spirits, mother, and not be **lonesome** because I'm not at home"* (Charles Dickens). ***Solitary*** often stresses physical isolation that is self-imposed: *I thoroughly enjoyed my **solitary** dinner.*

ambiguous   ambiguous, equivocal, vague

These adjectives mean lacking clarity, especially by being open to a variety of interpretations. ***Ambiguous*** indicates the presence of two or more possible meanings: *"It was impossible to tell from his **ambiguous** expression whether he knew what was happening"* (Paul Theroux). Something ***equivocal*** is unclear or misleading: *"The polling had a complex and **equivocal** message for potential female candidates"* (David S. Broder). What is ***vague*** is expressed in indefinite form or reflects imprecision of thought: *"**Vague** . . . forms of speech . . . have so long passed for mysteries of science"* (John Locke).

amuse   amuse, entertain, divert, regale

These verbs refer to activities that provide pleasure or enjoyment. ***Amuse*** can suggest the idle pleasure derived from a pastime: *I **amused** myself with a game of solitaire.* It can also suggest the enjoyment of something humorous or laughable: *The antics of the little dog **amused** the children.* ***Entertain*** often implies a pleasure actively pursued by the imagination or through play: ***entertained** herself with thoughts of what the weekend would bring; children **entertaining** themselves with games and puppets.* It also refers to the enjoyment derived from artistic performance: *has been **entertaining** audiences with his stories and music for many years.* ***Divert*** implies distraction from worry, boredom, or low spirits: *"I had* *neither Friends or Books to **divert** me"* (Richard Steele). To **regale** is to entertain with something that causes great mirth: *"He loved to **regale** his friends with tales about the many memorable characters he had known as a newspaperman"* (David Rosenzweig).

anger   **anger, rage, fury, ire, wrath, resentment, indignation**

These nouns denote varying degrees of marked displeasure. **Anger,** the most general, is strong and often heated displeasure: *shook her fist in **anger**; retorted in **anger** at the insult; tried to suppress his **anger** over the treatment he had received.* **Rage** and **fury** imply intense, explosive, often destructive emotion: *smashed the glass in a fit of **rage**; lashed out in **fury** at the lies her opponent had spread.* **Ire** is a term for anger most frequently encountered in literature: *"The best way to escape His **ire** / Is, not to seem too happy"* (Robert Browning). **Wrath** applies especially to a powerful anger that seeks vengeance or punishment: *"The public's **wrath** had been stirred by passage of a bill in 1816 raising representatives' pay from $6 to $15 per day"* (Ronald P. Formisano). **Resentment** refers to indignant smoldering anger generated by a sense of grievance: *deep **resentment** among the workers that eventually led to a strike.* **Indignation** is righteous anger at something wrongful, unjust, or evil: *"public **indignation** about takeovers causing people to lose their jobs"* (Allan Sloan).

angry   **angry, furious, indignant, irate, ireful, mad, wrathful**

These adjectives mean feeling or showing marked displeasure: *an **angry** retort; a **furious** scowl; an **indignant** denial; **irate** protesters; **ireful** words; **mad** at a friend; a **wrathful** tyrant.*

annihilate   **annihilate, exterminate, extinguish, obliterate**

These verbs mean to destroy completely: ***annihilated** the enemy's fortifications; **exterminated** the cockroaches in the house; criticism that **extinguished** my enthusiasm; a computer virus that **obliterated** the data on the hard drive.*

annoy   **annoy, irritate, bother, irk, vex, provoke, aggravate, peeve, rile**

These verbs mean to disturb or trouble a person, evoking moderate anger. **Annoy** refers to mild disturbance caused by an act that tries one's patience: *The sound of the printer **annoyed** me.* **Irritate** is somewhat stronger: *I was **irritated** by their constant interruptions.* **Bother** implies imposition: *In the end, his complaining just **bothered** the supervisor.* **Irk** connotes a wearisome quality: *The city council's inactivity **irked** the community.* **Vex** applies to situations arousing irritation, frustration, or perplexity: *They were **vexed** at having to wait so long for a response. This problem has **vexed** scientists for many years.* **Provoke** implies strong and often deliberate incitement to anger: *His behavior **provoked** me to reprimand the whole team.* **Aggravate** is a less formal equivalent: *"Threats only served to **aggravate** people in such cases"* (William Makepeace Thackeray). **Peeve,** also somewhat informal, suggests a querulous, resentful response to a mild disturbance: *Your flippant answers* **peeved** *me.* To **rile** is to upset and to stir up: *It* **riled** *me to have to listen to such lies.*

answer   answer, respond, reply, retort

These verbs relate to action taken in return to a stimulus. **Answer, respond,** and **reply,** the most general, all mean to speak, write, or act in response: *Please* **answer** *my question. Did you expect the President to* **respond** *personally to your letter? The opposing team scored three runs; the home team* **replied** *with two of their own.* **Respond** also denotes a reaction, either voluntary (*A bystander* **responded** *to the victim's need for help*) or involuntary (*She* **responded** *in spite of herself to the antics of the puppy*). To **retort** is to answer verbally in a quick, caustic, or witty manner: *She won the debate by* **retorting** *sharply to her opponent's questions.*

apparent   apparent, clear, clear-cut, distinct, evident, manifest, obvious, patent, plain

These adjectives mean readily seen, perceived, or understood: *angry for no* **apparent** *reason; a* **clear** *danger;* **clear-cut** *evidence of tampering; a* **distinct** *air of hostility; worry that was* **evident** *in his features;* **manifest** *pleasure;* **obvious** *errors;* **patent** *advantages; making my meaning* **plain.**

appreciate   appreciate, value, prize, esteem, treasure, cherish

These verbs mean to have a highly favorable opinion of someone or something. **Appreciate** applies especially to high regard based on critical assessment, comparison, and judgment: *As immigrants, they* **appreciated** *their newfound freedom.* **Value** implies high regard for the importance or worth of the object: *"In principle, the modern university* **values** *. . . the free exchange of ideas"* (Eloise Salholz). **Prize** often suggests pride of possession: *"the nonchalance* **prized** *by teen-agers"* (Elaine Louie). **Esteem** implies respect: *"If he had never* **esteemed** *my opinion before, he would have thought highly of me then"* (Jane Austen). **Treasure** and **cherish** stress solicitous care and affectionate regard: *We* **treasure** *our freedom. "They seek out the Salish Indian woman . . . to learn the traditions she* **cherishes***"* (Tamara Jones).

argue   argue, quarrel, wrangle, squabble, bicker

These verbs denote verbal exchange involving disagreement or conflict. To **argue** is to present reasons or facts in order to persuade someone of something: *"I am not* **arguing** *with you—I am telling you"* (James McNeill Whistler). It is also often used of more heated exchanges: *The couple* **argued** *for hours over who was at fault.* **Quarrel** denotes angry, often ongoing conflict: *The band* **quarreled** *with their manager over money.* It can also refer to continuing disputes of a public or professional nature: *"Experts still* **quarrel** *about the ultimate cause of Alzheimer's* [disease]*"* (Geoffrey Cowley). **Wrangle** refers to loud, contentious argument: *"audiences . . . who can be overheard* **wrangling** *about film facts in* *restaurants and coffee houses*" (Sheila Benson). ***Squabble*** and ***bicker*** both suggest sharp, persistent, bad-tempered infighting, often of a petty nature: "*A nobility of warriors . . . they **squabbled** endlessly on political matters, resolving the problems of dynastic succession with one bloodbath after another*" (Carlos Fuentes). *The senators **bickered** about adjustments to the tax proposal for weeks.*

ask

ask, question, inquire, query, interrogate, examine, quiz

These verbs mean to seek to gain or elicit information from another: ***Ask*** is the most neutral term: *We **asked** the police officer for directions. The coach **asked** me what was wrong.* ***Question*** implies careful or methodical asking: *The prosecutor **questioned** the witness on several key points.* ***Inquire*** often suggests a polite or formal request: *We **inquired** whether the hotel had laundry service. The chairman **inquired** how best to secure the information.* ***Query*** usually suggests settling a doubt: *The proofreader **queried** the author on the spelling of a name.* ***Interrogate*** applies especially to official and often aggressive questioning: *The detectives **interrogated** the suspects for several hours.* ***Examine*** refers particularly to close and detailed questioning to ascertain a person's knowledge or qualifications: *The committee **examined** each candidate separately.* ***Quiz*** denotes the informal examination of students: *The teacher **quizzed** the pupils on the multiplication table.*

assent

assent, agree, accede, acquiesce, consent, concur, subscribe

These verbs denote acceptance of another's views, proposals, or actions. To ***assent*** is to give an affirmative response, as to a proposal or request: "*He argued point by point that* [the queen] *knew of the plot, approved of it, **assented** to it*" (John Guy). ***Agree*** suggests an assent that is given in recognition of shared interests or as a result of persuasive argument: *They **agreed** to most of our proposed modifications but balked at any changes to the schedule.* ***Accede,*** in contrast, implies that one person or group has yielded to the other: "*She did **accede** to one of her mother's wishes: she wore a white dress*" (Bill Turque). ***Acquiesce*** suggests passive assent because of inability or unwillingness to oppose: *I **acquiesced** in their decision despite my misgivings.* ***Consent*** implies voluntary agreement, especially from one with the authority to say no: *The patient refused to **consent** to any further treatment.* ***Concur*** suggests that one has independently reached the same conclusion as another: "*I **concurred** with our incumbent in getting up a petition against the Reform Bill*" (George Eliot). ***Subscribe*** indicates hearty approval: "*I am contented to **subscribe** to the opinion of the best-qualified judge of our time*" (Sir Walter Scott).

attack

attack, assail, storm, assault, batter, beset

These verbs, drawn from military activity, mean in their figurative senses to act forcefully or aggressively toward someone or something. ***Attack*** applies especially to hostile verbal criticism: *reviews that **attacked** the film for its senseless violence; **attacked** the ruling as detrimental to business interests.* ***Assail*** suggests repeated forceful attacks: *Critics **assailed** the author's second novel.* ***Storm*** refers

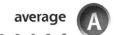

to a sudden sweeping attempt to overwhelm or win over: *"After triumphantly* **storming** *the country,* [the President] *is obliged to storm Capitol Hill"* (The Economist). *Assault* and *batter* can suggest relentless attack or debilitating force: *"We are all* **assaulted** *by so many messages battering us from the outside every hour of the day that our capacity for listening to our own inner voices is often drowned out"* (Harvey Cox). *Beset* suggests beleaguerment from all sides: *"Rural and suburban areas have been* **beset** *by white-tailed deer gnawing shrubbery and crops, spreading disease"* (Andrew C. Revkin).

attribute   attribute, ascribe, impute, credit, assign, refer

These verbs mean to consider as resulting from or belonging to a person or thing. *Attribute* and *ascribe,* often interchangeable, have the widest application: *The historian discovered a new symphony* **attributed** *to Mozart. The museum displayed an invention* **ascribed** *to the 15th century.* **Impute** is often used in laying guilt or fault to another: *"We usually* ascribe *good; but* **impute** *evil"* (Samuel Johnson). *Credit* usually refers to the acknowledgment of another for an accomplishment or contribution: *"Some excellent remarks were made on immortality, but mainly borrowed from and* **credited** *to Plato"* (Oliver Wendell Holmes, Sr.). *Assign* and *refer* are often used to classify or categorize: *Program music as a genre is usually* **assigned** *to the Romantic period. "A person thus prepared will be able to* **refer** *any particular history he takes up to its proper place in universal history"* (Joseph Priestley).

authentic   authentic, bona fide, genuine, real, true, unquestionable

These adjectives mean not counterfeit or copied: *an* **authentic** *painting by Monet; a* **bona fide** *transfer of property;* **genuine** *crabmeat; a* **real** *diamond;* **true** *courage; an* **unquestionable** *antique.*

average   average, medium, mediocre, middling, fair,
acceptable, indifferent, tolerable

These adjectives indicate a middle position on a scale of evaluation. *Average* and *medium* apply to what is midway between extremes and imply both sufficiency and lack of distinction: *a novel of* **average** *merit; a digital recording of* **medium** *quality.* **Mediocre** and *middling* stress the undistinguished aspect of what is average: *"The caliber of the students . . . has gone from* **mediocre** *to above average"* (Judy Pasternak); *"Every writer creates weak,* **middling** *and strong work"* (Frank Conroy). What is *fair* or *acceptable* is satisfactory or moderately good but has room for improvement: *a* **fair** *chance of winning; an* **acceptable** *grade on the test.* *Indifferent* means neither good nor bad and suggests a detached or resigned acceptance of such a status: *"Burningham was an* **indifferent** *student at every school he attended . . . and he preferred to be out of doors"* (Andrea Cleghorn). Something *tolerable* is good enough under the circumstances, but barely: *"Tennyson . . . suffered . . . from illness fears, particularly of going blind, though he lived into his eighties with* **tolerable** *eyesight"* (Carla Cantor).

aware
aware, cognizant, conscious, sensible, awake
These adjectives mean having knowledge or discernment of something. *Aware* implies knowledge gained through one's own perceptions or by means of outside information: *became **aware** of a cooling in their relationship; was not **aware** that the legislation passed*. *Cognizant* is a formal equivalent of *aware*: "*Our research indicates that the nation's youth are **cognizant** of the law*" (Jerry D. Jennings). *Conscious* emphasizes the inner workings of the mind or the direct experience of the senses as opposed to knowledge gained through information: "*Was Darwin really **conscious** of what he had done as he wrote his last professional lines?*" (Stephen Jay Gould); "*She was clearly **conscious** of the beauty of the night, its stars and sharp cold*" (Oliver La Farge). *Sensible* implies knowledge gained through intellectual perception: "*I am **sensible** that the mention of such a circumstance may appear trifling*" (Henry Hallam). To be *awake* is to be fully alert to something: "*He was as much **awake** to the novelty of attention in that quarter as Elizabeth herself could be*" (Jane Austen).

base
base, basis, foundation, ground, groundwork
These nouns all pertain to what underlies and supports. *Base* is used broadly in both literal and figurative contexts: *the wide **base** of the pyramid; a party seeking to expand its power **base***. *Basis* is used in a nonphysical sense: "*Healthy scepticism is the **basis** of all accurate observation*" (Arthur Conan Doyle). *Foundation* often stresses firmness of support for something of relative magnitude: "*Our flagrant disregard for the law attacks the **foundation** of this society*" (Peter D. Relic). *Ground* is used figuratively, especially in the plural, to mean a justifiable reason: ***grounds** for divorce*. *Groundwork* usually has the sense of a necessary preliminary: "*It [the Universal Declaration of Human Rights] has laid the **groundwork** for the world's war crimes tribunals*" (Hillary Rodham Clinton).

baseless
baseless, groundless, idle, unfounded, unwarranted
These adjectives mean being without a basis or foundation in fact: *a **baseless** accusation; **groundless** rumors; **idle** gossip; **unfounded** suspicions; **unwarranted** jealousy*.

beautiful
beautiful, lovely, pretty, handsome, comely, fair
All these adjectives apply to what excites aesthetic admiration. *Beautiful* is most comprehensive and applies to mental appreciation as well as sensual delight: *a **beautiful** child; a **beautiful** painting; a **beautiful** mathematical proof*. *Lovely* also has wide application but stresses sensual enjoyment or emotional response over critical faculties: *a **lovely** fragrance; the **lovely** feel of silk; greeted us with a **lovely** smile*. What is *pretty* is beautiful in a delicate or graceful way: *a **pretty** face; a **pretty** song; a **pretty** dress*. *Handsome* stresses poise and dignity of form and proportion: *a **handsome**, oak-paneled library*. "*She is very pretty, but not so extraordinarily **handsome***" (William Makepeace Thackeray). *Comely* suggests

wholesome physical attractiveness: *"Mrs. Hurd is a large woman with a big, **comely**, simple face"* (Ernest Hemingway). ***Fair*** emphasizes freshness or purity: *"In the highlands, in the country places, / Where the old plain men have rosy faces, / And the young **fair** maidens / Quiet eyes"* (Robert Louis Stevenson).

begin   begin, start, commence, launch, initiate, inaugurate

These verbs mean to take the initial step in doing something. ***Begin*** and ***start*** are the most general: *The conductor **began** the program with a medley of waltzes. We **started** our journey in Montreal.* ***Commence*** is a more formal term and often implies that what is beginning is something of seriousness or importance: *"ceremoniously brandishing the scalpel with which he was about to **commence** the apprentice's first lesson in anatomy"* (John Gregory Brown). ***Launch*** suggests beginning something with energy and expectation: *She looked for a job that could **launch** her career as a journalist.* ***Initiate*** applies to taking the first steps in a process or procedure: *I **initiated** a lawsuit against the driver who hit my car.* ***Inaugurate*** often connotes a formal beginning: *"The exhibition **inaugurated** a new era of cultural relations"* (Serge Schmemann).

beginning   beginning, birth, dawn, genesis, nascence, rise

These nouns denote the initial stage of a developmental process: *the **beginning** of a new era in technology; the **birth** of the industrial economy; the **dawn** of civilization; the **genesis** of quantum mechanics; the **nascence** of classical sculpture; the **rise** and decline of an ancient city-state.*
Antonym: end

behavior   behavior, conduct, bearing, deportment, comportment, demeanor

These nouns all pertain to a person's actions as they constitute a means of evaluation by others. ***Behavior*** is the most general: *The children were on their best **behavior**.* ***Conduct*** applies to actions considered from the standpoint of morality and ethics: *"Life, not the parson, teaches **conduct**"* (Oliver Wendell Holmes, Jr.). ***Bearing*** often carries with it the implication of social standing or position: *"It was evident from his **bearing** that he belonged to the country's ruling élite"* (Amitav Ghosh). ***Deportment*** and ***comportment*** pertain more narrowly to actions measured by a prevailing code of social behavior: *"the alleged decline in standards of **deportment**—a significant issue for an institution that prided itself on turning out 'gentlemen'"* (Jerome Karabel); *"Would I see a different person, or merely the same one governed by different conventions of **comportment** . . . accoutrement, and dress?"* (Witold Rybczynski). ***Demeanor*** suggests outward appearance that manifests inward emotion or character: *"The Beth I saw now was not only nimble-footed, but her **demeanor** was exuberant and self-assured"* (Rachel Simon).

belligerent **belligerent, bellicose, pugnacious, combative**

These adjectives mean having or showing an eagerness to fight. *Belligerent* refers to a tendency to hostile behavior: *A **belligerent** reporter badgered the politician.* *Bellicose* describes a warlike or hostile manner or temperament: *"Madison, far from being pushed into war by a **bellicose** Congress, had to drag his own hesitant party into it"* (Garry Wills). *Pugnacious* suggests a natural disposition to fight: *A good litigator needs a **pugnacious** intellect.* *Combative* implies an eagerness to fight or resist: *The senator made a **combative** defense of his record during the debate.*

benevolent **benevolent, charitable, eleemosynary, philanthropic**

These adjectives mean of, concerned with, providing, or provided by charity: *a **benevolent** fund; a **charitable** foundation; **eleemosynary** relief; **philanthropic** contributions.*

blemish **blemish, imperfection, fault, defect, flaw**

These nouns denote loss or absence of perfection. A *blemish* is something thought to mar the appearance or character of a thing: *"Industry in art is a necessity—not a virtue—and any evidence of the same, in the production, is a **blemish**"* (James McNeill Whistler). *Imperfection* and *fault* apply more comprehensively to any deficiency or shortcoming: *"A true critic ought to dwell rather upon excellencies than **imperfections**"* (Joseph Addison); *"Each of us would point out to the other her most serious **faults,** and thereby help her to remedy them"* (Anna Howard Shaw). *Defect* denotes a serious functional or structural shortcoming: *"Ill breeding . . . is not a single **defect,** it is the result of many"* (Henry Fielding). A *flaw* is an imperfection that may be hidden or of apparent insignificance but that often has serious consequences: *Experiments revealed a very basic **flaw** in the theory.*

block **block, hide, obscure, obstruct, screen, shroud**

These verbs mean to cut off from sight: *a tree that **blocked** the view; a road **hidden** by brush; mist that **obscured** the mountain peak; skyscrapers **obstructing** the sky; a fence that **screens** the alley; a face **shrouded** by a heavy veil.*

boast **boast, brag, crow, vaunt**

These verbs all mean to speak with pride, often excessive pride, about oneself or something related to oneself. *Boast* is the most general: *"We confide [that is, have confidence] in our strength, without **boasting** of it; we respect that of others, without fearing it"* (Thomas Jefferson). *Brag* implies exaggerated claims and often an air of insolent superiority: *He **bragged** about his grades.* *Crow* stresses exultation and often loud rejoicing: *No candidate should **crow** until the votes have been counted.* *Vaunt* suggests ostentatiousness and lofty extravagance of expression: *"He did not **vaunt** of his new dignity, but I understood he was highly pleased with it"* (James Boswell).

boil   boil, simmer, seethe, stew

These verbs mean, both literally and figuratively, to stir up or agitate. To **boil** is to heat a liquid until it churns with bubbles. Figuratively it pertains to intense agitation, often from anger: *She **boiled** with rage at the insult.* **Simmer** denotes gentle cooking just at or below the boiling point. Figuratively it refers to a state of slow, contained ferment: *Plans were **simmering** in his mind. The employees **simmered** with resentment over the cut in benefits.* To **seethe** is to boil steadily and vigorously. Its figurative usage can suggest vigorous activity or passionate emotion: *"The arc lamp's cone of light **seethes** with winged insects"* (Claire Davis). *"The city had . . . been **seething** with discontent"* (John R. Green). **Stew** refers literally to slow boiling and figuratively to a persistent but not violent state of agitation: *"They don't want a man to fret and **stew** about his work"* (William H. Whyte, Jr.).

border   border, edge, margin, verge, brink, rim

These nouns refer to the line that marks the outside limit of something, such as a surface or shape, or to the area just inside such a line. **Border** can refer to either the line (*a fence along the **border** of the property*) or the adjacent area (*a frame with a wide **border***). **Edge** refers to the bounding line formed by the continuous convergence of two surfaces (*sat on the **edge** of the wall*) or to an outer line or limit (*a leaf with serrated **edges**; stopped at the **edge** of the water*). **Margin** generally refers to a strip that runs along an edge or border: *the **margin** of the page; the grassy **margins** of a path.* A **verge** is an extreme terminating line or edge: *the sun's afterglow on the **verge** of the horizon.* Figuratively it indicates a point at which something is likely to begin or to happen: *an explorer on the **verge** of a great discovery.* **Brink** denotes the edge of a steep place: *stood on the **brink** of the cliff.* In an extended sense it indicates the likelihood or imminence of a sudden change: *on the **brink** of falling in love.* **Rim** most often denotes the edge of something circular or curved: *a cup with a chipped **rim**; the **rim** of a basketball goal; lava issuing from the **rim** of the crater.*

boring   boring, monotonous, tedious, irksome, tiresome

These adjectives refer to what is so lacking in interest as to cause mental weariness. Something that is **boring** fails to hold one's interest or attention, often resulting in listlessness or impatience: *I had never read such a **boring** book.* What is **monotonous** bores because of lack of variety: *"There is nothing so desperately **monotonous** as the sea"* (James Russell Lowell). **Tedious** suggests dull slowness, long-windedness, or stultifying routine: *"It was a life full of the **tedious**, repetitive tasks essential to small-press publishing and grassroots organizing"* (Jan Clausen). **Irksome** emphasizes the irritation or resentment provoked by something tedious: *"I know and feel what an **irksome** task the writing of long letters is"* (Edmund Burke). Something **tiresome** fatigues because it seems to be interminable or to be marked by unremitting sameness: *"What a **tiresome** being is a man who is fond of talking"* (Benjamin Jowett).

brave

brave, courageous, fearless, intrepid, bold, audacious, valiant, valorous, mettlesome, plucky, dauntless, undaunted

These adjectives mean having or showing courage under difficult or dangerous conditions. *Brave,* the least specific, is frequently associated with an innate quality: *"Familiarity with danger makes a **brave** man **braver**"* (Herman Melville). *Courageous* implies an inner strength that draws on principle or purpose as well as character: *"The millions of refugees who have resettled here . . . are **courageous** . . . people who stood for something"* (Robert E. Pierre and Paul Farhi). *Fearless* emphasizes absence of fear and a willingness or even eagerness to take risks: *"world-class [boating] races for **fearless** loners willing to face the distinct possibility of being run down, dismasted, capsized, attacked by whales"* (Jo Ann Morse Ridley). *Intrepid* suggests a fearlessness tempered by steadfast determination: *"The great snowpeaks of the Himalayas isolated their communities from all but the most **intrepid** outsiders"* (Mark Abley). *Bold* stresses readiness to meet danger or difficulty and often a tendency to seek it out: *"If we shrink from the hard contests where men must win at the hazard of their lives . . . then the **bolder** and stronger peoples will pass us by"* (Theodore Roosevelt). *Audacious* implies daring, brazen, or extravagant boldness: *"the **audacious** belief that many answers to questions of cosmic origin and evolution may be within their grasp"* (John Noble Wilford). *Valiant* and *valorous* suggest heroic bravery in service of a noble cause: *"the **valiant** English who had defended their land for a thousand years"* (Willie Morris); *"The other hostages [will] never forget her calm, confident, **valorous** work"* (William W. Bradley). *Mettlesome* stresses spirit and love of challenge: *"her horse, whose **mettlesome** spirit required a better rider"* (Henry Fielding). *Plucky* emphasizes spirit and heart in the face of unfavorable odds: *"He couldn't abide the typical children's-book scenario of a **plucky** hero or heroine triumphing over adversity"* (Christine M. Heppermann). *Dauntless* and *undaunted* imply unflagging courage and a refusal to be dismayed: *"So faithful in love, and so **dauntless** in war, / There never was knight like the young Lochinvar"* (Sir Walter Scott); *"Death and sorrow will be the companions of our journey. . . . We must be united, we must be **undaunted**, we must be inflexible"* (Winston S. Churchill).

brawl

brawl, donnybrook, fracas, fray, free-for-all, melee, scrap, scrape, scuffle

These nouns denote a noisy, disorderly, and often violent quarrel or fight: *a barroom **brawl**; a vicious legal **donnybrook**; a **fracas** among prison inmates; eager for the **fray**; a **free-for-all** in the schoolyard; police plunging into the **melee**; a **scrap** between opposing players; a **scrape** that took place at the mall; a **scuffle** that broke out in the courtroom.*

breach	**breach, infraction, violation, transgression, trespass, infringement**

These nouns denote an act or instance of breaking a law or regulation or of failing to fulfill a duty, obligation, or promise. ***Breach*** and ***infraction*** are the least specific; when applied to lawbreaking they may imply a relatively minor offense, but they are also widely used in nonlegal contexts: *Revealing the secret would be a **breach** of trust. Their behavior amounted to an **infraction** of the unwritten social code.* ***Violation*** generally applies to the breaking of an explicit law or rule (*a traffic **violation**; a **violation** of international law*); it can also imply a failing to follow a moral or ethical standard: *a **violation** of human rights; a **violation** of one's privacy.* ***Transgression*** and ***trespass*** most often apply to divine or moral law: *"She had said that the **transgression** was all the more shocking because the official was charged with enforcing federal laws against sexual harassment"* (Jane Mayer and Jill Abramson); *"The act of torture is such an extreme **trespass** against the laws of war that it may seem beside the point to wonder whether any other forms of wrongdoing have been carried out"* (Elaine Scarry). ***Infringement*** is most frequently used to denote encroachment on another's rights: *"Necessity is the plea for every **infringement** of human freedom"* (William Pitt the Younger).

break	**break, crack, fracture, burst, splinter, shatter, smash**

These verbs mean to separate or cause to separate into parts or pieces, either by the sudden application of force or by the pressure of internal stress. ***Break*** is the most general: *That delicate ornament will **break** easily. The window was **broken** by vandals. The bag held so many heavy things that it **broke**.* To ***crack*** is to break without dividing into parts: *The building's foundation **cracked** during the earthquake. By bumping against the counter I **cracked** the coffeepot, but it didn't leak.* ***Fracture*** applies to a break or crack in a rigid body: *Heat and pressure caused the bedrock to **fracture**. She **fractured** her hip in the accident.* ***Burst*** implies a sudden coming apart, especially from internal pressure: *The pipe **burst** during the cold snap. The child **burst** the balloon with a pin.* ***Splinter*** implies splitting into long, thin, sharp pieces: *The boat's hull **splintered** when it hit the reef. The crowbar **splintered** the jamb, and the door opened.* To ***shatter*** is to break into many scattered pieces: *The icicle **shattered** when it landed on the front steps. The ball **shattered** the window upon impact.* ***Smash*** stresses force of blow or impact and suggests complete destruction: *I dropped the vase, and it **smashed** into pieces. The storm winds **smashed** the orchard trees, ruining the harvest.*

bright	**bright, brilliant, radiant, lustrous, lambent, luminous, incandescent, effulgent**

These adjectives refer to what emits or reflects light. ***Bright*** is the most general: ***bright** sunshine; a **bright** white shirt.* ***Brilliant*** implies intense brightness and often suggests sparkling or gleaming light: ***brilliant** floodlights; a **brilliant** gemstone.* Something ***radiant*** emits or seems to emit light in rays: *a **radiant** sunrise; a table set with **radiant** crystal.* A ***lustrous*** object reflects an agreeable sheen: *thick, lustrous hair. Lambent* applies to a soft, flickering light: *"its tranquil streets, bathed in the lambent green of budding trees"* (James C. McKinley). *Luminous* especially refers to something that glows in the dark: *a luminous watch dial. Incandescent* stresses burning brilliance: *fireworks exploding in incandescent colors. Effulgent* suggests splendid radiance: *"The crocus, the snowdrop, and the effulgent daffodil are considered bright harbingers of spring"* (John Gould).

brood brood, dwell, fret, mope, worry

These verbs mean to turn something over in the mind moodily and at length: *brooding about his decline in popularity; dwelled on her defeat; fretted over the loss of his job; moping about his illness; worrying about the unpaid bills.*

bulge bulge, balloon, belly, jut, project, protrude

These verbs mean to curve, spread, or extend outward past the normal or usual limit: *a wallet bulging with money; a clown's pants that ballooned at the waist; a sail bellying in the wind; a boulder jutting from the hillside; a deck that projected from the house in back; eyes protruding from their sockets in astonishment.*

burden burden, affliction, albatross, cross, millstone, trial, tribulation

These nouns denote something onerous or troublesome: *the burden of a guilty conscience; considered the television an affliction that destroyed the spirit of community; a poorly built home that became his albatross; an unhappy marriage that became a cross to bear; a routine duty that turned into a millstone; a troublemaker who is a trial to the teacher; suffered many tribulations in rising from poverty.*

burn burn, scorch, singe, sear, char

These verbs mean to injure or alter by means of intense heat or flames. *Burn,* the most general, applies to the effects of exposure to a source of heat or to something that can produce a similar effect: *burned the muffins in the oven; skin burned by the wind and sun. Scorch* involves superficial burning that discolors or damages the texture of something: *scorched the shirt with the iron. Singe* specifies superficial burning and especially the removal of hair or feathers from a carcass before cooking: *singed his finger lighting the match; plucked and singed the chicken before roasting it. Sear* applies to rapid superficial burning using high heat: *seared the meat in a hot skillet.* To *char* is to reduce a substance to carbon or charcoal by partial burning: *trees charred by the forest fire.*

business business, industry, commerce, trade, traffic

These nouns apply to forms of activity that have the objective of supplying products or services for a fee. *Business* pertains broadly to commercial, financial, and industrial activity, and more narrowly to specific fields or firms engaging in this activity: *a company that does business over the Internet; went into the software consulting business; owns a dry-cleaning business. Industry* entails the production and manufacture of goods or commodities, especially on a large scale: *the computer* **industry.** **Commerce** and **trade** refer to the exchange and distribution of goods or commodities: *laws regulating interstate* **commerce**; *involved in the domestic fur* **trade.** **Traffic** pertains in particular to businesses engaged in the transportation of goods or passengers: *renovated the docks to attract shipping* **traffic.** The word may also suggest illegal trade: *discovered a brisk* **traffic** *in stolen goods.*

calculate

calculate, compute, reckon, figure

These verbs refer to the use of mathematical methods to determine a result. *Calculate,* the most comprehensive, often implies a relatively high level of abstraction or procedural complexity: **calculated** *the average test score for each class;* **calculated** *the comet's orbit from a series of observed positions.* **Compute** applies to possibly lengthy arithmetic operations; like **calculate,** it may imply the use of a mechanical or electronic device: *data used in* **computing** *the gross national product;* **computed** *a value for each of the variables.* **Reckon** and **figure** suggest the use of simple arithmetic: **reckoned** *the number of hours before her departure; trying to* **figure** *my share of the bill.*

calm

calm, peaceful, placid, serene, tranquil

These adjectives denote absence of excitement or disturbance: **calm** *acceptance of the inevitable; a* **peaceful** *hike through the scenic hills; a soothing,* **placid** *temperament; spent a* **serene,** *restful weekend at the lake; hoped for a more* **tranquil** *life in the country.*

care

care, charge, custody, keeping, supervision, trust

These nouns refer to the function of watching, guarding, or overseeing: *left the keys in my* **care**; *has* **charge** *of the library's rare books; took* **custody** *of the author's papers; left the canary in the neighbors'* **keeping**; *assumed* **supervision** *of the students; documents committed to the bank's* **trust.**

careful

careful, alert, attentive, heedful, mindful, vigilant, watchful

These adjectives mean giving close or cautious attention: *were* **careful** *not to get their shoes muddy;* **alert** *to any change in the patient's condition;* **attentive** *to her driving;* **heedful** *of potential danger;* **mindful** *of his health; a* **vigilant** *customs official; a* **watchful** *babysitter.*

careless

careless, heedless, thoughtless, inadvertent

These adjectives apply to people who perform actions marked by insufficient care or attention or to the actions themselves. *Careless* often implies negligence or casual indifference: *"It is natural for* **careless** *writers to run into faults they never think of"* (George Berkeley). **Heedless** can suggest willful or reckless disregard: *"She . . . watched the top of the hill for someone drunk or* **heedless** *coming over it in part of her lane"* (Andre Dubus). **Thoughtless** applies to actions taken without due consideration; it frequently implies lack of concern for others: *"a* *thoughtless remark about the war that will worry an already worried child*" (Kristin Henderson). **Inadvertent** implies unintentional lack of care or attention: "*For the deterrence theorists, the greatest worry was **inadvertent** war, a cataclysm that might follow from misperception*" (Eliot A. Cohen).

catch catch, enmesh, ensnare, entangle, entrap, snare, trap

These verbs mean to take in and hold as if by using bait or a lure: *caught in a web of lies; **enmeshed** in the dispute; **ensnared** an unsuspecting customer; became **entangled** in her own contradictions; **entrapped** by a convincing undercover agent; **snared** by false hopes; **trapped** into incriminating himself.*

celebrity celebrity, hero, luminary, name, notable, personage

These nouns refer to a widely known person: *a social **celebrity**; the **heroes** of science; a theatrical **luminary**; a big **name** in sports; a **notable** of the concert stage; a **personage** in the field of philosophy.*

chance chance, random, casual, haphazard, desultory

These adjectives apply to what is determined not by deliberation but by happenstance. **Chance** stresses lack of intention or premeditation: *a **chance** meeting with a friend.* **Random** implies the absence of a specific pattern or objective: *at the mercy of **random** events.* **Casual** stresses the indiscriminate or unpredictable nature of chance events: "*the **casual** mutation of one of your liver cells from normal to cancerous*" (John Barth). **Haphazard** implies a carelessness or lack of control: "*If unmarried significant others are invited to participate in the family support groups at all, it tends to be on a **haphazard,** informal basis*" (Kristin Henderson). **Desultory** denotes a sporadic or aimless sequence of events: "*I lay on a shared cot listening to **desultory** gunfire*" (Jan Clausen).

charm charm, beguile, bewitch, captivate, enchant, entrance, fascinate

These verbs mean to delight so much that one's interest and attention are held: *a performance that **charmed** the theater critic; a gourmet meal that **beguiles** discerning diners; a musical comedy that **bewitched** its audience; a novel that **captivates** its readers; a child who **enchanted** his grandparents; music that **entrances** its listeners; a celebrity who **fascinated** her interviewer.*
Antonym: repel

chief chief, foremost, leading, main, primary, prime, principal

These adjectives refer to what is first in rank, importance, or influence: *his **chief** concern; the **foremost** scholar in her field; the **leading** cause of heart disease; the **main** building on campus; the **primary** purpose of the legislation; a **prime** example of wasteful spending; the **principal** figures in the plot.*

choice   **choice, selection, alternative, option, preference**

These nouns denote something chosen or available for choosing: *Choice* and *selection* are the most general: *My first **choice** was too costly. My **selection** from the menu turned out to be delicious.* Both words can refer to a range of things available for choosing: *You have a wide **choice** of colors. The store had a good **selection** of wines. **Alternative** emphasizes choice between two possibilities or courses of action: "Since the days of Thomas A. Edison, the auto industry has been trying to make a credible **alternative** to the internal combustion engine"* (Danny Hakim). ***Option** is often used of a choice that requires careful consideration: The legislature outlined many tax **options**. **Preference** indicates a choice based on one's values, bias, or predilections: We were offered our **preference** of appetizers.*

cold   **cold, arctic, chilly, cool, frigid, frosty, gelid, glacial, icy**

These adjectives mean marked by a low or an extremely low temperature: ***cold** air; an **arctic** climate; a **chilly** day; **cool** water; a **frigid** room; a **frosty** morning; **gelid** seas; **glacial** winds; **icy** hands.*
Antonym: hot

comfortable   **comfortable, easy, cozy, snug**

These adjectives mean affording ease of mind or body. ***Comfortable** implies the absence of sources of pain or distress: wears **comfortable** clothes.* The word may also suggest peace of mind: *felt **comfortable** with the decision. **Easy** denotes freedom from worry or stress: an **easy** life with plenty of time for leisure activities. **Cozy** suggests homey and reassuring comforts: sat in a **cozy** nook near the fire. **Snug** brings to mind the image of a warm, secure, compact shelter: children **snug** in their beds.*

common   **common, ordinary, familiar**

These adjectives describe what is generally known or frequently encountered. ***Common** applies to what takes place often, is widely used, or is well known: The botanist studied the **common** dandelion.* The term also implies coarseness or a lack of distinction: *My wallet was stolen by a **common** thief. **Ordinary** describes something usual that is indistinguishable from others, sometimes derogatorily: A ballpoint pen is adequate for **ordinary** purposes. The critic gave the **ordinary** performance a mediocre review. **Familiar** applies to what is well known or quickly recognized: Most children can recite **familiar** nursery rhymes.*

complete   **complete, finish, close, end, conclude, terminate**

These verbs mean to bring to a natural or proper stopping point. ***Complete** and **finish** suggest the final stage in an undertaking: "Nothing worth doing is completed in our lifetime"* (Reinhold Niebuhr). *"Give us the tools, and we will **finish** the job"* (Winston S. Churchill). ***Close** and **end** both imply bringing something ongoing to a conclusion: The band **closed** the concert with an encore. We **ended***

the meal with fruit and cheese. **End** can also mean putting a stop to something, often with finality: *"Many advocates say* [putting] *laptops in schools is a promising way to* **end** *the digital divide between the races"* (Char Simons); *"It left him more exposed than ever, forcing him to* **end** *the career he loved"* (Molly Worthen). **Conclude** is more formal than **close** and **end**: *The author* **concluded** *the article by restating the major points.* **Terminate** suggests reaching an established limit: *The playing of the national anthem* **terminated** *the station's broadcast for the night.* It also indicates the dissolution of a formal arrangement: *The firm* **terminated** *my contract yesterday.*

complex

complex, complicated, intricate, involved, tangled

These adjectives mean having parts so interconnected as to hamper comprehension or perception of the whole. **Complex** implies a combination of many interwoven parts: *The composer transformed a simple folk tune into a* **complex** *set of variations.* **Complicated** stresses a relationship of parts that affect each other in elaborate, often obscure ways: *The party's* **complicated** *platform confused many voters.* **Intricate** refers to a pattern of intertwining parts that is difficult to follow or analyze: *"No one could soar into a more* **intricate** *labyrinth of refined phraseology"* (Anthony Trollope). **Involved** implies a close but confusing interconnection between many different parts: *The movie's plot was criticized as being too* **involved.** **Tangled** strongly suggests the random twisting of many parts: *"Oh, what a* **tangled** *web we weave, / When first we practice to deceive!"* (Sir Walter Scott).

confirm

confirm, corroborate, substantiate, authenticate, validate, verify

These verbs mean to establish or support the truth, accuracy, or genuineness of something. **Confirm** implies the establishment of certainty or conviction: *The information* **confirmed** *our worst suspicions.* To **corroborate** something is to strengthen or uphold the evidence that supports it: *The witness is expected to* **corroborate** *the plaintiff's testimony.* To **substantiate** is to establish by presenting solid or reliable evidence: *"What I shall say can be* **substantiated** *by the sworn testimony of witnesses"* (Mark Twain). To **authenticate** something is to establish its genuineness, as by expert testimony or documentary proof: *Never purchase an antique before it has been* **authenticated.** **Validate** refers to establishing the validity of something, such as a theory, claim, or judgment: *The divorce* **validated** *my parents' original objection to the marriage.* **Verify** implies proving by comparison with an original or with established fact: *The bank refused to cash the check until the signature was* **verified.**

conflict

conflict, discord, strife, contention, dissension, clash

These nouns refer to a state of disagreement and disharmony. **Conflict** has the broadest application: *a* **conflict** *of interests; a* **conflict** *between the demands of* *work and family.* **Discord** is a lack of harmony often marked by bickering and antipathy: *a long history of family **discord**; a summit marred by **discord** among the leaders.* **Strife** usually implies an open struggle, often destructive, between rivals or factions: *marital **strife** that ended in divorce; ethnic tensions that were a constant source of **strife**.* **Contention** suggests a dispute in the form of heated debate or quarreling: *lively **contention** among the candidates.* **Dissension** implies difference of opinion that disrupts unity within a group: *rampant **dissension** among the staff.* **Clash** involves irreconcilable ideas or interests: *a **clash** between tradition and modernity; a **clash** of egos.*

contain   contain, hold, accommodate

These verbs mean to have or be able to have within. **Contain** means to have within or have as a part or constituent: *The box **contained** emergency medical supplies. The book **contains** some amusing passages.* **Hold** stresses capacity for containing: *The gas tank **holds** 15 gallons when full.* **Accommodate** refers to capacity for holding comfortably: *The restaurant **accommodates** 50 customers.*

contaminate   contaminate, befoul, foul, poison, pollute, taint

These verbs mean to make dirty or impure: *Pesticides **contaminated** the lake. Mud **befouled** his shoes. Noxious fumes **foul** the air. Farm runoff **poisoned** the fish. Exhaust **polluted** the air. Improper storage **tainted** the food.*

contemporary   contemporary, contemporaneous, simultaneous, synchronous, concurrent, coincident, concomitant

These adjectives mean existing or occurring at the same time. **Contemporary** and **contemporaneous** often refer to historical or indefinite time periods, with **contemporary** used more often of persons and **contemporaneous** of events and facts: *The composer Salieri was **contemporary** with Mozart. A rise in interest rates is often **contemporaneous** with an increase in inflation.* **Simultaneous** suggests a briefer or more definite moment in time and often implies deliberate coordination: *The activists organized **simultaneous** demonstrations in many major cities.* **Synchronous** refers to related events that occur together, usually as part of a process or design: *"A single, **synchronous** flowering and seed-bearing . . . is common in bamboos in both the Old World and the New"* (David G. Campbell). **Concurrent** refers to events or conditions, often of a parallel nature, that coexist in time: *The administration had to deal with **concurrent** crises on three different continents.* **Coincident** applies to events occurring at the same time without implying a relationship: *"The resistance to the Pope's authority . . . is pretty nearly **coincident** with the rise of the Ottomans"* (John Henry Newman). **Concomitant** is used of concurrent events, one of which is viewed as attendant on the other: *"The sweetness of naturally low-calorie fruits, vegetables, and grains may be enhanced without a **concomitant** increase in caloric content"* (Leona Fitzmaurice).

continual **continual, continuous, ceaseless, constant, incessant, perpetual, eternal, perennial**

These adjectives mean occurring without stopping or occurring repeatedly over a long period of time. ***Continual*** is often restricted to what is intermittent or repeated at intervals: *The **continual** banging of the shutter in the wind gave me a headache.* But it can also imply a lack of interruption, the focus of ***continuous*** and ***ceaseless***: *The fugitive was living in a state of **continual** fear. The police put the house under **continuous** surveillance. We listened to the **ceaseless** babble of the stream.* ***Constant*** stresses steadiness or persistence and unvarying nature: *The **constant** ticking of the clock lulled him to sleep.* ***Incessant*** adds to ***constant*** the suggestion of annoying repetition: *The dog's **incessant** barking kept him up all night.* ***Perpetual*** emphasizes both steadiness and duration: *One side of the moon is in **perpetual** darkness.* ***Eternal*** refers to what is everlasting, especially to what is seemingly without temporal beginning or end: *"That freedom can be retained only by the **eternal** vigilance which has always been its price"* (Elmer Davis). ***Perennial*** describes existence that goes on year after year, often with the suggestion of self-renewal: *The candidates discussed the **perennial** problem of urban poverty.*

correct **correct, rectify, remedy, redress, revise, amend**

These verbs mean to make right what is wrong. ***Correct*** refers to eliminating faults, errors, or defects: *I **corrected** the spelling mistakes. The new design **corrected** the flaws in the earlier version.* ***Rectify*** stresses the idea of bringing something into conformity with a standard of what is right: *"It is dishonest to claim that we can **rectify** racial injustice without immediate cost"* (Mari J. Matsuda). ***Remedy*** involves removing or counteracting something considered a cause of harm, damage, or discontent: *He took courses to **remedy** his abysmal ignorance.* ***Redress*** refers to setting right something considered immoral or unethical and usually involves some kind of recompense: *"They said he had done very little to **redress** the abuses that the army had committed against the civilian population"* (Daniel Wilkinson). ***Revise*** suggests change that results from careful reconsideration: *The agency **revised** its safety recommendations in view of the new findings.* ***Amend*** implies improvement through alteration or correction: *"Whenever [the people] shall grow weary of the existing government, they can exercise their constitutional right of **amending** it, or their revolutionary right to dismember or overthrow it"* (Abraham Lincoln).

correspond **correspond, conform, harmonize, coincide, accord, agree**

These verbs all indicate a compatibility between people or things. ***Correspond*** refers to similarity in form, nature, function, character, or structure: *"Scientific statements may or may not **correspond** to the facts of the physical world"* (George Soros). ***Conform*** stresses correspondence in essence or basic characteristics, sometimes to an ideal or established standard: *"Home was the place where I was forced to **conform** to someone else's image of who and what I should be"* (bell hooks). *Harmonize* implies the combination or arrangement of elements in a pleasing whole: *The print on the curtains **harmonized** with the striped sofa.* ***Coincide*** stresses exact agreement: *"His interest happily **coincided** with his duty"* (Edward A. Freeman). ***Accord*** implies harmony, unity, or consistency, as in essential nature: *"The creed [upon which America was founded] was widely seen as both progressive and universalistic: It **accorded** with the future, and it was open to all"* (Everett Carll Ladd). ***Agree*** may indicate mere lack of incongruity or discord, although it often suggests acceptance of ideas or actions and thus accommodation: *We finally **agreed** on a price for the house.*

criticize   criticize, censure, condemn, denounce, decry

These verbs mean to express an unfavorable judgment. ***Criticize*** can mean merely to evaluate without necessarily finding fault; however, usually the word implies the expression of disapproval: *formed a panel to **criticize** the students' works; was angry when his parents **criticized** the way he dressed.* ***Censure*** refers to the often formal pronouncement of strong criticism: *"[He] **censured** from the pulpit what many others have welcomed as a much-needed religious awakening"* (John Edgar Wideman). ***Condemn*** usually applies to harsh moral judgment: *"The wrongs which we seek to **condemn** and punish have been so calculated, so malignant and so devastating that civilization cannot tolerate their being ignored because it cannot survive their being repeated"* (Robert H. Jackson). ***Denounce*** and ***decry*** imply public proclamation of condemnation or repudiation: *"Fictionalizing in the writing of biography . . . has been largely **denounced** by critics . . . and teachers"* (Margaret Bush); *"The worship of the senses has often, and with much justice, been **decried**"* (Oscar Wilde).

crush   crush, mash, smash, squash

These verbs mean to press forcefully so as to reduce to a pulpy mass: ***crushed** the rose geranium leaves; **mashed** the sweet potatoes; **smashed** the bamboo stems with a hammer; **squashed** the wine grapes.*

cry   cry, weep, wail, bawl, keen, sob, blubber

These verbs mean to express strong emotion, such as grief, misery, or pain, by shedding tears or making inarticulate sounds. ***Cry*** and ***weep*** both involve the shedding of tears: *"She **cried** without trying to suppress any of the noisier manifestations of grief and confusion"* (J. D. Salinger); *"I **weep** for what I'm like when I'm alone"* (Theodore Roethke). ***Wail*** and ***bawl*** refer to loud sustained utterance, as in grief, misery, or fear: *"The women . . . began to **wail** together; they mourned with shrill cries"* (Joseph Conrad); *"Her voice was always hoarse. Her Dad said this was because she had **bawled** so much when she was a baby"* (Carson McCullers). ***Keen*** refers more specifically to wailing and lamentation for the dead: *"It is the wild Irish women **keening** over their dead"* (George A. Lawrence). ***Sob*** describes weeping or a mixture of broken speech and weeping marked by convulsive breathing or gasping: *"**sobbing** and crying, and wringing her hands* *as if her heart would break*" (Laurence Sterne). **Blubber** refers to noisy shedding of tears accompanied by broken or inarticulate speech: "*When he drew out what had been a fiddle, crushed to morsels in the greatcoat, he* **blubbered** *aloud*" (Emily Brontë).

dark

dark, dim, murky, dusky, shady, shadowy

These adjectives indicate the absence of light or clarity. **Dark,** the most widely applicable, can refer to a lack or near lack of illumination (*a* **dark** *night*), deepness of shade or color (**dark** *brown*), somberness (*a* **dark** *mood*), or immorality (*a* **dark** *past*). **Dim** means having or producing little light (**dim** *shadows; a* **dim** *light bulb*) and further suggests lack of sharpness or clarity: "*the terrible* **dim** *faces known in dreams*" (Carson McCullers); "*tales now* **dim** *and half forgotten*" (Jane Stevenson). **Murky** refers to a thick or clouded darkness: "*Dolphins use sonar beams to navigate the* **murky** *depths of the ocean*" (Tim Hilchey). Like **dim**, it is also used of what is indistinct or uncertain: "*Modern warfare is* **murky,** *and with no clear frontlines, the distinction between combat and support can become meaningless*" (Kristin Henderson). **Dusky** suggests a subdued half-light: "*The* **dusky** *night rides down the sky, / And ushers in the morn*" (Henry Fielding). It can also refer to deepness or darkness of color: "*A* **dusky** *blush rose to her cheek*" (Edith Wharton). **Shady** refers literally to what is sheltered from light, especially sunlight (*a* **shady** *grove of pines*) or figuratively to what is of questionable honesty (**shady** *business deals*). **Shadowy** also implies obstructed light (*an ill-lit,* **shadowy** *street*) but may refer to what is indistinct or little known: "*[He] retreated from the limelight to the* **shadowy** *fringe of music history*" (Charles Sherman). It can also refer to something that seems to lack substance and is mysterious or sinister: *a* **shadowy** *figure in a black cape.*

deceive

deceive, mislead, delude, dupe, hoodwink, bamboozle

These verbs mean to cause someone to believe something untrue, usually with an ulterior motive in mind. **Deceive**, the most general, stresses the deliberate misrepresentation of what one knows to be true: "*We are inclined to believe those whom we do not know, because they have never* **deceived** *us*" (Samuel Johnson). To **mislead** is to direct toward a wrong conclusion, as by the use of half-truths or obfuscation; it is often but not always intentional: "*Writing for young people may tempt authors to oversimplify technical information, which may* **mislead** *or confuse the reader*" (Margaret Bush). **Delude** can imply a deception so thorough as to foster belief that is not merely misplaced but often irrational; it may also imply a strong dose of wishful thinking: "*We* [working parents] **delude** *ourselves into believing that extended day programs, baby sitters and latchkey arrangements fill the bill*" (Ann Symonds). To **dupe** is to play upon another's susceptibilities or naïveté: *The shoppers were* **duped** *by false advertising.* **Hoodwink** and the informal **bamboozle** refer to deception by hoaxing, trickery, or artful persuasion: "*Worst of all . . . the orchestra manager . . . has somehow* **hoodwinked** *me with his courtly southern manner into signing another multiyear contract*" (Arnold

Steinhardt). *"Perhaps if I wanted to be understood or to understand I would bamboozle myself into belief, but I am a reporter"* (Graham Greene).

decide   decide, determine, settle, rule, conclude, resolve

These verbs mean to come to a decision about. ***Decide*** has the broadest range: *The judge will **decide** the case on its merits. We **decided** to postpone our vacation for a week.* ***Determine*** has a similar range but often involves somewhat narrower issues: *The doctor **determined** the cause of the infection. The jury will **determine** the fate of the defendant.* ***Settle*** stresses finality of decision: *"The lama waved a hand to show that the matter was finally **settled** in his mind"* (Rudyard Kipling). ***Rule*** implies that the decision is handed down by someone in authority: *The committee **ruled** that changes in the curriculum should be implemented.* ***Conclude*** suggests that a decision, opinion, or judgment has been arrived at after careful consideration: *She **concluded** that the criticism was unjust.* ***Resolve*** stresses the exercise of choice in making a firm decision: *I **resolved** to lose weight.*

decrease   decrease, lessen, reduce, dwindle, abate, diminish, subside

These verbs mean to become smaller or less or to cause something to become smaller or less. ***Decrease*** and ***lessen*** have the most general application: *saw the plane descend as its speed **decreased**; vowed to **decrease** government spending; an appetite that **lessened** as the disease progressed; restrictions aimed at **lessening** the environmental impact of off-road vehicles.* ***Reduce*** often emphasizes bringing down in size, degree, or intensity: ***reduced** the heat once the mixture reached a boil; workers who **refused** to reduce their wage demands.* ***Dwindle*** suggests decreasing bit by bit to a vanishing point: *savings that **dwindled** away in retirement.* ***Abate*** stresses a decrease in amount or intensity and suggests a reduction of excess: *a blustery wind that **abated** toward evening; increased the dosage in an effort to **abate** the pain.* ***Diminish*** stresses the idea of loss or depletion: *a breeze that arose as daylight **diminished**; a scandal that **diminished** the administration's authority.* ***Subside*** implies a falling away to a more normal level or state: *floodwaters that did not **subside** until days after the storm passed; anger that **subsided** with understanding.*

defeat   defeat, beat, conquer, rout, vanquish

These verbs mean to triumph over an adversary: ***defeated** the opposing team by fourteen points; **beat** her competitor in the race for first place; **conquered** the enemy after a long battle; **routed** all opposition due to a brilliant strategy; **vanquished** the marauding army in a surprise attack.*

defend   defend, protect, guard, preserve, shield, safeguard

These verbs mean to make or keep safe from danger, attack, or harm. ***Defend*** implies repelling or being ready to repel an attack: ***defended** the border against the enemy; responded quickly to **defend** his reputation.* ***Protect*** often suggests keeping something safe by coming between it and any threat of harm or injury: *soldiers who **protected** stores from looters; wore sunglasses to **protect** her eyes.*

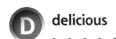

Guard suggests keeping watch: *guarded the house against intruders.* To **preserve** something is to protect it from future harm or alteration: *a group that purchases land to* **preserve** *it from commercial development.* **Shield** suggests providing a barrier against something dangerous or destructive: *a hedge that* **shielded** *the house from winter winds.* **Safeguard** implies the vigilant protection of something of great value or importance: *The Bill of Rights* **safeguards** *our individual liberties.*

delicious

delicious, delectable, luscious, scrumptious, toothsome, yummy

These adjectives mean very pleasing to the sense of taste: *a **delicious** pâté; **delectable** raspberries; **luscious** chocolate bonbons; a **scrumptious** peach; a **toothsome** apple; **yummy** fudge.*

depressed

depressed, blue, dejected, despondent, disconsolate, dispirited, downcast, downhearted

These adjectives mean affected or marked by low spirits: ***depressed** by the loss of his job; lonely and **blue** in a strange city; is **dejected** but trying to look cheerful; the **despondent** supporters of the losing candidate; the **disconsolate** leaders of a besieged town; **dispirited** workers facing a plant closing; looked **downcast** after his defeat; a **downhearted** patient who welcomed visitors.*

describe

describe, narrate, recite, recount, relate, report

These verbs mean to tell the facts, details, or particulars of something in speech or in writing: ***described** the accident; **narrated** their travel experiences; an explorer **reciting** her adventures; a mercenary **recounting** his exploits; **related** the day's events; **reported** what she had seen.*

desire

desire, covet, crave, want, wish

These verbs mean to have a strong longing for: ***desire** peace; **coveted** the new car; **craving** fame and fortune; **wanted** a drink of water; **wished** that she had gone to the beach.*

destroy

destroy, raze, demolish, ruin, wreck

These verbs mean to cause the complete ruin or wreckage of something or someone. ***Destroy, raze,*** and ***demolish*** can all imply reduction to ruins or even complete obliteration: *"I saw the best minds of my generation **destroyed** by madness"* (Allen Ginsberg); *"**raze** what was left of the city from the surface of the earth"* (John Lothrop Motley). *The prosecutor **demolished** the opposition's argument.* **Ruin** usually implies irretrievable harm but not necessarily total destruction: *"You will **ruin** no more lives as you ruined mine"* (Arthur Conan Doyle). To **wreck** is to ruin in or as if in a violent collision: *"The Boers had just **wrecked** a British military train"* (Arnold Bennett). When **wreck** is used in referring to the ruination of a person or of his or her hopes or reputation, it implies irreparable shattering: *"Coleridge, poet and philosopher **wrecked** in a mist of opium"* (Matthew Arnold).

dexterous   dexterous, deft, adroit, handy, nimble

These adjectives refer to skill and ease in performance. *Dexterous* implies physical or mental agility: *dexterous fingers; a dexterous debater.* *Deft* suggests quickness, sureness, neatness, and lightness of touch: *deft strokes; a deft turn of phrase.* *Adroit* implies ease and natural skill, especially in challenging situations: *an adroit skier; an adroit negotiator.* *Handy* suggests a more modest aptitude, principally in manual work: *handy with tools.* *Nimble* stresses quickness and lightness in physical or mental performance: *nimble feet; nimble wits.*

difference   difference, dissimilarity, unlikeness, divergence, variation, distinction, discrepancy

These nouns refer to a lack of correspondence or agreement. *Difference* is the most general: *differences in color and size; a difference of degree but not of kind.* *Dissimilarity* and *unlikeness* often suggest a wide or fundamental difference: *the dissimilarity between human and computer language; attracted to each other by their very unlikeness.* However, *dissimilarity* is also used to emphasize the points of difference between things that are otherwise alike or comparable: *an analysis of the dissimilarities between the two sets of data.* *Divergence* can denote a difference resulting from a branching or separation; alternatively, it can indicate a range of difference within a category: *the growing divergence between British and American English; a large group with a divergence of opinions on the subject.* *Variation* occurs between things of the same class or species; often it refers to a modification of something original, prescribed, or typical: *variations in temperature; a variation of a familiar technique.* *Distinction* often means a difference in detail determinable only by close inspection: *the distinction between "good" and "excellent."* A *discrepancy* is a difference between things that should correspond or match: *a discrepancy between his words and his actions.*

diligent   diligent, industrious, conscientious, assiduous, sedulous

These adjectives suggest steady attention and effort that is undertaken to accomplish something. *Diligent* connotes steady, meticulous attention to an ongoing job or task: *"[They] have won international renown for their diligent efforts to track down software bugs"* (Hiawatha Bray). *Industrious* implies energetic and productive application, often to a large or important endeavor: *"Madison's and Jefferson's vision of an agrarian republic made up largely of industrious farmers who marketed their burgeoning surpluses abroad"* (Drew R. McCoy). *Conscientious* carries with it the implication of energetic attentiveness springing from dutifulness or a sense of responsibility: *"a studious, conscientious public servant authentically dedicated to improving the welfare of his fellow human beings"* (Randall Bennett Woods). *Assiduous* and the less common *sedulous* emphasize untiring exertion and an earnestness of purpose: *"How do Olympians acquire [talent]? Were they born with it, or did they develop it through assiduous practice?"* (Steve Olson); *"the sedulous pursuit of legal and moral principles"* (Ernest van den Haag).

dirty **dirty, filthy, grimy, grubby, squalid**

These adjectives apply to what is unclean, impure, or unkempt: *dirty clothes; filthy rags; grimy hands; an old grubby stove; a squalid apartment.*

disappear **disappear, evanesce, evaporate, fade, vanish**

These verbs mean to pass out of sight or existence: *a skyscraper disappearing in the fog; time seeming to evanesce; courage evaporating; memories fading away; hope slowly vanishing.*

dishonest **dishonest, lying, untruthful, deceitful, mendacious**

These adjectives mean lacking honesty or truthfulness. **Dishonest** is the least specific: *a dishonest reply; a dishonest business executive; had been dishonest with myself.* **Lying** conveys a blunt accusation of falsehood: *a lying witness whose testimony fell apart under cross-examination.* **Untruthful** is a softer term and often suggests evasiveness or distortion rather than outright lies: *published an untruthful account of the incident.* **Deceitful** implies misleading by falsehood or by concealment of the truth: *deceitful advertising.* **Mendacious** is more formal than **lying**, and suggests a chronic inclination toward untruth: *a mendacious, power-hungry politician.*

disparage **disparage, denigrate, belittle, depreciate**

These verbs mean to minimize the value or importance of someone or something. **Disparage** implies a critical or dismissive attitude often accompanied by disrespect: *"Leaders who wouldn't be caught dead making religious or ethnic slurs don't hesitate to disparage the 'godless' among us"* (Daniel C. Dennett). **Denigrate** often adds a note of contempt: *"elitist music critics who denigrated jazz by portraying it as inferior to the classical tradition"* (Tyler Stovall). **Belittle** means to reduce someone or something to a lowly status, often in an arrogant or hurtful manner: *"those who would mock and belittle others simply on the basis of their physical appearance"* (Tyler Dilts). **Depreciate** implies the assignment of a low estimation of value or worth, though the judgment it expresses is generally less disdainful than in the previous terms: *"[19th-century American] literature was still mainly subservient to English models and depreciated as secondhand and second rate"* (Chronology of American Literature).

disposition **disposition, temperament, character, personality, nature**

These nouns refer to the combination of qualities that identify a person. **Disposition** is approximately equivalent to prevailing frame of mind or spirit: *"A patronizing disposition always has its meaner side"* (George Eliot). **Temperament** applies broadly to the sum of emotions, habits, and beliefs that affect or determine a person's actions and reactions: *"She is . . . of a very serene and proud and dignified temperament"* (H.G. Wells). **Character** can refer to a defining or distinguishing set of personal traits: *"Whatever his peculiarities of character and* *outlook, he was far and away the most conversable person in our circle*" (Andrew Ryan). More often, though, it emphasizes a person's positive moral and ethical qualities: "*Education has for its object the formation of character*" (Herbert Spencer). **Personality** is the sum of distinctive traits that give a person individuality: *an outgoing, friendly* **personality**. **Nature** denotes native or inherent qualities: "*It is my habit,—I hope I may say, my* **nature**,*—to believe the best of people*" (George W. Curtis).

distort

distort, twist, deform, contort, warp

These verbs mean to alter form or character, usually disadvantageously. To **distort** is to change the physical shape of something, as by torsion or exaggerating certain features, or to misconstrue the meaning of something: "*The human understanding is like a false mirror, which, receiving rays irregularly,* **distorts** *and discolors the nature of things*" (Francis Bacon). **Twist** applies to distortion of form or meaning: **twisted** *his mouth in pain; accused me of* **twisting** *her words.* **Deform** refers to change that disfigures and often implies the loss of desirable qualities such as beauty: *erosion that* **deformed** *the landscape.* **Contort** implies violent change that produces unnatural or grotesque effects: *rage that* **contorted** *that actor's face; conclusions that were* **contorted** *by a desire for a favorable outcome.* **Warp** can refer to turning from a flat or straight form or from a true course or direction: *floorboards that had* **warped** *over the years; judgment* **warped** *by prejudice.*

distribute

distribute, apportion, divide, dispense, dole, deal, ration

These verbs mean to give out in portions or shares. **Distribute** is the least specific: *The government* **distributed** *land to settlers.* **Apportion** and **divide** imply giving out portions, often equal, on the basis of a plan or purpose: *The funds were* **apportioned** *to each school district. The estate will be* **divided** *among the heirs.* **Dispense** stresses the careful determination of portions, often according to measurement or weight: *The pharmacist* **dispensed** *the medication.* **Dole,** often followed by **out,** implies careful, usually sparing measurement of portions. It can refer to the distribution of charity: *The city* **doled out** *surplus milk to the needy.* **Deal** implies orderly, equitable distribution, often piece by piece: *I* **dealt** *five cards to each player.* **Ration** refers to equitable division in limited portions of scarce, often necessary, items: *The government* **rationed** *fuel during the war.*

dull

dull, colorless, drab, humdrum, lackluster, pedestrian, stodgy, uninspired

These adjectives mean lacking in liveliness, charm, or surprise: *a* **dull**, *uninteresting performance; a* **colorless** *and unimaginative person; a* **drab** *and boring job; a* **humdrum** *conversation; a* **lackluster** *life; a* **pedestrian** *movie plot; a* **stodgy** *dinner party; an* **uninspired** *lecture.*
Antonym: lively

earn   **earn, deserve, merit, rate, win**

These verbs mean to gain as a result of one's behavior or effort: *earns a large salary; deserves our thanks; a suggestion that merits consideration; an event that rates a mention in the news; a candidate who won wide support.*

easy   **easy, simple, facile, effortless**

These adjectives mean requiring little effort or posing little if any difficulty. *Easy* applies to tasks that require little effort: *a recipe that is easy to prepare; an easy hike around the lake.* *Simple* implies a lack of complexity that facilitates understanding or performance: *instructions that are simple to follow; a simple problem that took little time to fix.* *Facile* stresses fluency stemming from preparation: *the author's facile use of literary conventions.* Often, though, the word implies glibness or insincerity, superficiality, or lack of care: *a supervisor's facile dismissal of an employee suggestion.* *Effortless* refers to performance in which the application of great strength or skill makes the execution seem easy: *wrote effortless prose.*

eat   **eat, consume, devour, ingest**

These verbs mean to take food into the body by the mouth: *ate a hearty dinner; greedily consumed the sandwich; hyenas devouring their prey; whales ingesting krill.*

effect   **effect, consequence, result, outcome, upshot**

These nouns denote an occurrence, situation, or condition that is produced by a cause or agent. *Effect* stresses the idea of influence or alteration: *a drug whose main effect is to lower hypertension; increased erosion that was the effect of deforestation.* A *consequence* follows naturally or logically from its cause: *a broken wrist that was the consequence of a fall; a reduction in crime that was the consequence of better policing.* A *result* is viewed as the end product of the operation of the cause: *improved his grades as a result of better study habits; an experiment with an unexpected result.* An *outcome* more strongly implies finality and may suggest the resolution of a complex or lengthy process: *The trial's outcome might have changed if the defendant had testified.* An *upshot* is a decisive result, often of the nature of a climax: "*The upshot of the matter . . . was that she showed both of them the door*" (Robert Louis Stevenson).

element   **element, component, constituent, factor, ingredient**

These nouns denote one of the individual parts of which a composite entity is made up: *the grammatical elements of a sentence; real estate as a component of wealth; a protein that is a constituent of a virus; analyzed the factors that led to the accident; a cake made of flour, eggs, and other ingredients.*

embarrass   **embarrass, abash, chagrin, discomfit, disconcert, faze**

These verbs mean to cause someone to feel self-conscious and uneasy: *were embarrassed by their child's tantrum; felt abashed at the disclosure of the error; will be chagrined if my confident prediction fails; was discomfited by the sudden* *personal question; is **disconcerted** by sarcastic remarks; refuses to be **fazed** by your objections.*

empty   empty, vacant, blank, void, vacuous

These adjectives mean without contents that could or should be present. ***Empty*** is the broadest and can apply to what lacks contents (*an **empty** box*), occupants (*an **empty** seat*), or substance (*an **empty** promise*). ***Vacant*** has a similar range of application, including lacking an occupant (*a **vacant** auditorium*), an incumbent (*a **vacant** position*), or something useful or substantial (*a **vacant** lot*); it can also refer to what is without intelligence or expression (*a **vacant** stare*). ***Blank*** applies specifically to the absence of writing or images on a surface (*a **blank** page; a **blank** screen*) and can extend to a lack of awareness or understanding (*a **blank** look*). ***Void*** emphasizes the utter degree to which something is lacking, whether physical (*a planet **void** of life*) or intangible (*a humdrum performance **void** of spirit or energy*). ***Vacuous*** describes what is lacking in substance, interest, or intelligence (***vacuous** entertainment; a **vacuous** personality*).

endanger   endanger, hazard, imperil, jeopardize, risk

These verbs mean to subject to danger, loss, or destruction: *erratic driving that **endangers** lives; **hazarded** his health by smoking; a forest **imperiled** by acid rain; costs that **jeopardized** profits; wouldn't **risk** her financial security.*

enmity   enmity, hostility, antagonism, animosity, animus, antipathy

These nouns refer to the feeling or expression of ill will toward another. ***Enmity*** is deep-seated hatred that seeks to oppose, harm, or defeat another: *"hardhat construction workers—symbols of blue-collar **enmity** toward the antiwar movement"* (Bill Turque). ***Hostility*** is similar to ***enmity*** but often suggests an angry reaction or vigilant opposition: *"The Court had demonstrated its **hostility** to affirmative action in several recent cases"* (Mari Matsuda & Charles Lawrence III). ***Antagonism*** often suggests mutual hostility: *"The **antagonism** between business—especially big industrial business—and environmentalists appeared to be a war that would never end"* (Lis Harris). ***Animosity*** and ***animus*** connote visceral emotion: *"Just beneath the surface of their civility . . . lurked a powerful **animosity** between Johnson and Kennedy"* (Nick Kotz); *"The examination became a forum in which [he] could vent his **animus** against the administration"* (Joseph A. McCartin). ***Antipathy*** is deep-seated aversion or repugnance: *a long-held **antipathy** to modern art.*

enormous   enormous, immense, huge, gigantic, colossal, mammoth, tremendous, gargantuan, vast

These adjectives describe what is extraordinarily large. ***Enormous*** suggests a marked excess beyond the norm in size, amount, or degree: *an **enormous** boulder.* ***Immense*** refers to boundless or immeasurable size or extent: *an **immense** sky.* ***Huge*** especially implies greatness of size or capacity: *a **huge** tanker.* ***Gigantic*** refers to size likened to that of a giant: *a **gigantic** redwood tree.* ***Colossal*** suggests a hugeness that elicits awe or taxes belief: *a valley ringed by* **colossal** *mountains.* **Mammoth** is applied to something of unwieldy hugeness: *"***mammoth** *stone fig-ures in . . . buckled eighteenth-century pumps, the very soles of which seem moun-tainously tall"* (Cynthia Ozick). **Tremendous** suggests awe-inspiring or fearsome size: *a* **tremendous** *waterfall.* **Gargantuan** stresses greatness of size or capacity and often suggests extravagance or excess: *"Dense schools of menhaden . . . slurp up enormous quantities of plankton and detritus like* **gargantuan** *vacuum cleaners"* (H. Bruce Franklin). **Vast** refers to greatness of extent, size, area, or scope, and is often applied to what inspires a sense of grandeur or awe: *"Another* **vast** *mountain of darkness rose, towering up like a wave that should engulf the world"* (J.R.R. Tolkien).

equipment equipment, gear, outfit, paraphernalia

These nouns denote the materials needed for a purpose such as a task or a journey: *hiking* **equipment**; *skiing* **gear**; *an explorer's* **outfit**; *a beekeeper's* **paraphernalia**.

erase erase, expunge, delete, cancel

These verbs mean to remove or invalidate something, especially something stored, recorded, or written down. To **erase** is to wipe or rub out, literally or figuratively: **erased** *the word from the blackboard;* **erased** *any hope of success.* **Expunge** implies thorough removal: *a performance that* **expunged** *doubts about his ability.* To **delete** is to remove matter from a manuscript or data from a computer application: **deleted** *expletives from the transcript;* **deleted** *the file with one keystroke.* **Cancel** refers to invalidating by or as if by drawing lines through something written: **canceled** *the postage stamp;* **canceled** *the reservation.*

evade evade, elude, avoid, eschew

These verbs mean to get or stay away from something or someone undesir-able. **Evade** implies adroit maneuvering and sometimes suggests dishonesty or irresponsibility: *tried to* **evade** *jury duty.* To **elude** is to get away from artfully: **eluded** *their pursuers.* **Avoid** suggests a prudent or deliberate effort to stay away from what is unpleasant, harmful, or disadvantageous: *took the back roads to* **avoid** *the heavy traffic; followed his doctor's advice to* **avoid** *strenuous exercise.* **Eschew** is a formal equivalent of **avoid**: *"***Eschew** *evil, and do good"* (King James Bible).

example example, instance, case, illustration, specimen

These nouns refer to what is representative of or serves to explain a larger group or class. An **example** is a typically representative part that demonstrates the character of the whole: *"Of the despotism to which unrestrained military power leads we have plenty of* **examples** *from Alexander to Mao"* (Samuel Eliot Mori-son). An **instance** is an example that is cited to prove or illustrate a point: *offered the statistics as an* **instance** *of why the penal system needed to be overhauled.* A **case** is an example belonging to a particular category: *a* **case** *of life imitating art.*

An *illustration* clarifies or explains: "[The author] *has provided an* ***illustration*** *of a first-rate experimental mind at work*" (Richard Bernstein). ***Specimen*** often denotes an individual, representative member of a group or class: *This poem is a fair* ***specimen*** *of her work.*

excel

excel, surpass, exceed, outdo, outstrip

These verbs mean to be greater or better than someone or something. To ***excel*** is to achieve a level higher than another or others: ***excelled*** *the other speakers in wit and eloquence.* To ***surpass*** is to go beyond another in performance, quality, or degree: *a marathoner who* ***surpassed*** *his previous record; a picture quality that far* ***surpassed*** *that of earlier models.* ***Exceed*** can refer to being superior to another (*an invention that* ***exceeds*** *all others in ingenuity*), to being greater than something (*a salary* ***exceeding*** *250 thousand dollars a year*), and to going beyond a proper limit (***exceed*** *one's authority*). ***Outdo*** and ***outstrip*** imply leaving another or others behind, as in a contest or competition: *Democrats and Republicans striving to* ***outdo*** *each other in patriotic fervor; a student who* ***outstripped*** *her classmates in academic honors.*

excessive

excessive, immoderate, intemperate, inordinate, extravagant, extreme

These adjectives mean exceeding a normal, usual, reasonable, or proper limit. ***Excessive*** has the widest range: ***excessive*** *drinking;* ***excessive*** *debt; an* ***excessive*** *amount of fat in the diet.* ***Immoderate*** and ***intemperate*** denote a lack of due moderation or restraint: ***immoderate*** *political views;* ***intemperate*** *personal remarks.* ***Inordinate*** adds to these words a sense of going beyond what is proper or deserved: ***inordinate*** *self-regard; took an* ***inordinate*** *time to reply.* ***Extravagant*** sometimes specifies lavish or unwise expenditure (***extravagant*** *gifts*); often it implies overstepping the bounds of reason or prudence (***extravagant*** *claims;* ***extravagant*** *speculation in the stock market*). ***Extreme*** suggests going far beyond what is normal, desirable, or generally acceptable: *an* ***extreme*** *diet; an* ***extreme*** *ideology.*

expect

expect, anticipate, hope, await

These verbs relate to the idea of looking ahead to something in the future. To ***expect*** is to look forward to the likely occurrence or appearance of someone or something: *"We should not* ***expect*** *something for nothing—but we all do and call it Hope"* (Edgar W. Howe). ***Anticipate*** sometimes refers to taking advance action, as to forestall or prevent the occurrence of something expected or to meet a wish or request before it is articulated: ***anticipated*** *the storm and locked the shutters.* The term can also refer to having a foretaste of something expected: *The police are* ***anticipating*** *trouble with rowdy fans after the game.* To ***hope*** is to look forward with desire and usually with a measure of confidence in the likelihood of gaining what is desired: *I* ***hope*** *to see you soon.* To ***await*** is to wait expectantly and with certainty: *She is eagerly* ***awaiting*** *your letter.*

explain   explain, elucidate, explicate, interpret, construe

These verbs mean to make the nature or meaning of something understandable. *Explain* is the most widely applicable: *The professor used a diagram to **explain** the theory of continental drift. The manual **explained** how the new software worked.* To ***elucidate*** is to throw light on something complex: *"Man's whole life and environment have been laid open and **elucidated**"* (Thomas Carlyle). ***Explicate*** implies detailed and usually learned and lengthy exploration or analysis: *"Ordinary language philosophers tried to **explicate** the standards of usage"* (Jerrold J. Katz). To ***interpret*** is to reveal the underlying meaning of something by the application of special knowledge or insight: *"A radiologist can **interpret** images made in Saudi Arabia and beamed to Boston, sending back a diagnosis within hours"* (Richard Saltus). ***Construe*** involves putting a particular construction or interpretation on something: *"I take the official oath today . . . with no purpose to **construe** the Constitution or laws by any hypercritical rules"* (Abraham Lincoln).

exquisite   exquisite, delicate, elegant, fine

These adjectives mean appealing to refined taste: *an **exquisite** wine; a **delicate** flavor; **elegant** handwriting; the **finest** embroidery.*

extricate   extricate, disengage, disentangle, untangle

These verbs mean to free from something that entangles: ***extricated** herself from an embarrassing situation; **disengaged** his attention from the television; sought to **disentangle** fact from fiction in the account; lawyers tasked with **untangling** the corporation's financial dealings.*

fair   fair, just, equitable, impartial, unprejudiced, unbiased, objective

These adjectives mean free from favoritism, self-interest, or preference in judgment. *Fair* is the most general: *a **fair** referee; a **fair** deal. **Just*** stresses conformity with what is legally or ethically right or proper: *"a **just** and lasting peace"* (Abraham Lincoln). ***Equitable*** implies justice dictated by reason, conscience, and a natural sense of what is fair: *an **equitable** distribution of gifts among the children.* ***Impartial*** emphasizes lack of favoritism: *"the cold neutrality of an **impartial** judge"* (Edmund Burke). ***Unprejudiced*** means without preconceived opinions or judgments: *an **unprejudiced** evaluation of the proposal.* ***Unbiased*** implies absence of a preference or partiality: *gave an **unbiased** account of her family problems.* ***Objective*** implies detachment that permits impersonal observation and judgment: *an **objective** jury.*

faithful   faithful, loyal, true, constant, fast, steadfast, staunch

These adjectives mean adhering firmly and devotedly to someone or something that elicits or demands one's fidelity. *Faithful* and *loyal* both suggest undeviating attachment, though *loyal* applies more often to political allegiance: *a **faithful** employee; a **loyal** citizen.* ***True*** implies steadiness, sincerity, and reliability:

remained **true** to her innermost beliefs. **Constant** stresses uniformity and invariability: *"But I am **constant** as the northern star"* (Shakespeare). **Fast** emphasizes firmness and closeness of attachment: *remained **fast** friends throughout their life.* **Steadfast** implies fixed, unswerving loyalty: *a **steadfast** ally.* **Staunch** even more strongly suggests unshakable attachment or allegiance: *a **staunch** supporter of the cause.*

famous **famous, celebrated, eminent, famed, illustrious, notable, noted, preeminent, renowned**

These adjectives mean widely known and esteemed: *a **famous** actor; a **celebrated** musician; an **eminent** scholar; a **famed** scientist; an **illustrious** judge; a **notable** historian; a **noted** author; a **preeminent** archaeologist; a **renowned** painter.*
***Antonym:* obscure**

fast **fast, rapid, swift, fleet, speedy, quick, expeditious**

These adjectives refer to something marked by great speed. **Fast** and **rapid** are often used interchangeably, though **fast** is more often applied to the person or thing in motion, and **rapid** to the activity or movement involved: *a **fast** runner; **rapid** strides.* **Swift** suggests smoothness and sureness of movement (*a **swift** current*), and **fleet**, lightness of movement (*The cheetah is the **fleetest** of animals*). **Speedy** refers to velocity (*a **speedy** train*) or to promptness or hurry (*a **speedy** resolution to the problem*). **Quick** most often applies to what takes little time or to what is prompt: *a **quick** snack; your **quick** reaction.* **Expeditious** suggests rapid efficiency: *sent the package by the most **expeditious** means.*

fat **fat, overweight, obese, corpulent, portly, stout, pudgy, rotund, plump, chubby**

These adjectives mean having an abundance and often an excess of flesh. **Fat** implies more weight than one desires or than is considered desirable by social norms: *was getting **fat** and decided to exercise.* **Overweight** conveys the sense that the weight is above a medical standard for age or height and may be unhealthy: *oversized garments for **overweight** customers.* Another word with medical connotations, **obese** means grossly overweight: *"a woman of robust frame . . . though stout, not **obese**"* (Charlotte Brontë). While **corpulent** also refers to conspicuous body weight, it is not always as judgmental a term as *obese: the **corpulent** figure of the seated Buddha.* **Portly** refers to bulk combined with a stately or imposing bearing: *"a **portly**, rubicund man of middle age"* (Winston Churchill). **Stout** denotes a thickset, bulky figure: *a painting of **stout** peasants.* **Pudgy** means short and fat: ***pudgy** fingers.* **Rotund** refers to the roundness of figure associated with a spreading midsection: *"this pink-faced **rotund** specimen of prosperity"* (George Eliot). **Plump** and **chubby** apply to a pleasing fullness of figure: *a **plump** little toddler; **chubby** cheeks.*

fatal

fatal, deadly, lethal, mortal

These adjectives apply to what causes or is likely to cause death. *Fatal* describes conditions, circumstances, or events that have already caused death or are virtually certain to do so in the future: *a **fatal** accident; a **fatal** illness.* ***Deadly*** means capable of killing or of being used to kill: *a **deadly** poison; a **deadly** weapon.* ***Lethal*** has a similar range, often with a suggestion of deliberate or calculated intent: *execution by **lethal** injection; the **lethal** technology of modern warfare.* ***Mortal*** describes a condition or action that produces death, typically in a context of combat: *a **mortal** wound; delivered a **mortal** blow.*

fear

fear, fright, dread, terror, horror, panic, alarm, trepidation, apprehension

These nouns denote the agitation and anxiety caused by the presence or imminence of danger. *Fear* is the most general term: *a morbid **fear** of snakes; was filled with **fear** as the car skidded off the road.* ***Fright*** is sudden, intense, usually momentary fear: *"Pulling open the door, she started back in **fright** at the unknown face before hers"* (Donna Morrissey). ***Dread*** is visceral fear, especially in anticipation of something dangerous or unpleasant: *felt a mounting **dread** as the battle approached; approached the oral exam with **dread**.* ***Terror*** is intense, overpowering fear: *"And now at the dead hour of the night . . . so strange a noise as this excited me to uncontrollable **terror**"* (Edgar Allan Poe). ***Horror*** is a combination of fear and aversion or repugnance: *reacted with **horror** to the news of the atrocities.* ***Panic*** is sudden frantic fear, often affecting many people at the same time: *The shoppers fled in **panic** at the sound of gunshots.* ***Alarm*** is anxious concern caused by the first realization of danger or a setback: *I watched with **alarm** as the sky darkened.* ***Trepidation*** and ***apprehension*** are more formal terms for dread: *"I awaited the X-ray afterward with **trepidation**"* (Atul Gawande); *"Now there were just the two of them . . . and they were headed for the hospital . . . and she was what calmed his **apprehension** and allowed him to be brave"* (Philip Roth).

field

field, bailiwick, domain, province, realm, sphere, territory, turf

These nouns denote an area of activity, thought, study, or interest: *the **field** of comparative literature; considers marketing to be her **bailiwick**; the **domain** of physics; the **province** of politics; the **realm** of constitutional law; a task within his assistant's **sphere**; the **territory** of historical research; bureaucrats interested only in protecting their **turf**.*

figure

figure, design, device, motif, pattern

These nouns denote an element or arrangement of elements in a decorative composition: *a tapestry with a floral **figure**; a rug with a geometric **design**; a brooch with a fanciful and intricate **device**; a scarf with a heart **motif**; fabric with a plaid **pattern**.*

flash flash, gleam, glint, sparkle, glitter, glisten, glimmer, twinkle, scintillate

These verbs mean to send forth light. *Flash* refers to a sudden and brilliant but short-lived outburst of light: *A bolt of lightning flashed across the horizon.* *Gleam* implies a transient or subdued light that often appears against a dark background: *"The light gleams an instant, then it's night once more"* (Samuel Beckett). *Glint* applies to briefly gleaming or flashing light: *"the fountain's silver-painted swan glinted in the moonlight"* (Kate Wheeler). *Sparkle* suggests a rapid succession of little flashes of high brilliance (*crystal glasses sparkling in the candlelight*), and *glitter,* a similar succession of even greater intensity (*jewels glittering in the display case*). To *glisten* is to shine with a sparkling luster: *The snow glistened in the dawn light.* *Glimmer* refers to faint, fleeting light: *"On the French coast the light / Gleams, and is gone; the cliffs of England stand, / Glimmering and vast, out in the tranquil bay"* (Matthew Arnold). To *twinkle* is to shine with quick, intermittent flashes or gleams: *"a few stars, twinkling faintly in the deep blue of the night sky"* (Hugh Walpole). *Scintillate* is applied to what flashes as if emitting sparks in a continuous stream: *"a dense, hoary mist of ammonium chloride . . . depositing minute scintillating crystals on the window-panes"* (Primo Levi).

flexible flexible, elastic, resilient, supple

These adjectives refer literally to what is capable of withstanding stress without damage and figuratively to what can undergo change or modification: *a flexible wire; flexible plans; an elastic rubber band; an elastic interpretation of the law; thin, resilient copper; a resilient temperament; supple suede; a supple mind.*

flow flow, current, flood, rush, stream, tide

These nouns denote something suggestive of running water, as in power of movement or abundance: *a flow of thought; the current of history; a flood of ideas; a rush of sympathy; a stream of complaints; a tide of immigration.*

follow follow, succeed, ensue, result

These verbs mean to come after something or someone. *Follow,* the most general, refers to people or things that come after another in time or order or as a consequence or result: *You go first, and we'll follow. He disregarded doctor's orders, and a relapse soon followed.* To *succeed* is to come next after another, especially in planned order determined by considerations such as rank, inheritance, or election: *The heir apparent succeeded to the throne.* *Ensue* and *result* are used only of events or conditions that follow another in time. *Ensue* usually applies to what is a consequence: *After the government was toppled, chaos ensued.* *Result* implies that what follows is caused by what has preceded: *Driving over the speed limit can result in a fine.*

foolish **foolish, absurd, fatuous, ludicrous, preposterous, ridiculous, silly**
These adjectives are applied to people or things that show an absence of good judgment or common sense: *a **foolish** expenditure of energy; an **absurd** idea that is bound to fail; **fatuous** optimism that does not take the real problem into account; dismissed her **ludicrous** criticism; a **preposterous** excuse that no one believed; offered a **ridiculous** explanation for his tardiness; a **silly** argument.*

forbid **forbid, ban, prohibit, proscribe**
These verbs mean to refuse to allow: *laws that **forbid** speeding; **banned** smoking in restaurants; rules that **prohibit** loitering; **proscribed** the importation of certain fruits.*
Antonym: **permit**

force **force, compel, coerce, oblige, obligate**
These verbs mean to cause one to follow a prescribed or dictated course against one's will. ***Force***, the most general, usually implies the exertion of physical power or the operation of circumstances that permit no options: *The driver was **forced** from his car at gunpoint. A downturn in the market **forced** us to sell.* ***Compel*** has a similar range but applies especially to the exertion of legal or moral authority: *The official was **compelled** to testify under the committee's subpoena power. I felt **compelled** by my conscience to return the money.* ***Coerce*** implies the application of pressure or threats in securing compliance: *"The technology exists to reduce or eliminate these emissions, but industry will not apply it unless **coerced**"* (Andrew Weil). ***Oblige*** implies the operation of authority, necessity, or moral or ethical considerations: *"Work consists of whatever a body is **obliged** to do"* (Mark Twain). ***Obligate*** applies when compliance is enforced by a legal contract or by the dictates of one's conscience or sense of propriety: *I am **obligated** to repay the loan.*

foretell **foretell, augur, divine, prophesy**
These verbs mean to tell about something beforehand by or as if by supernatural means: ***foretelling** the future; **augured** a scandal; **divined** the enemy's victory; **prophesying** a stock-market boom.*

forgive **forgive, pardon, excuse, condone**
These verbs mean to refrain from imposing punishment on an offender or demanding satisfaction for an offense. The first three can be used as conventional ways of offering apology. More strictly, to ***forgive*** is to grant pardon without harboring resentment: *"Children begin by loving their parents; as they grow older they judge them; sometimes they **forgive** them"* (Oscar Wilde). ***Pardon*** more strongly implies release from the liability for or penalty entailed by an offense: *After the revolution all political prisoners were **pardoned**.* To ***excuse*** is to pass over a mistake or fault without demanding punishment or redress: *"Valencia was incredibly generous to these deadbeats. She memorized their poetry and **excused** their bad behavior"* (David Sedaris). To ***condone*** is to overlook an

offense, usually a serious one, and often suggests tacit forgiveness: *Failure to protest the policy may imply a willingness to **condone** it.*

form

form, figure, shape, contour, profile

These nouns refer to the external outline of a thing. ***Form*** is the outline and structure of a thing as opposed to its substance: *the pointed **form** of a pyramid; a brooch in the **form** of a lovers' knot.* ***Figure*** refers usually to form as established by bounding or enclosing lines: *The cube is a solid geometric **figure**.* ***Shape*** can imply either two-dimensional outline or three-dimensional definition that indicates both outline and bulk or mass: *paper cutouts in the **shape** of flowers and stars; "He faced her, a hooded and cloaked **shape**"* (Joseph Conrad). ***Contour*** refers to the outline and often the surface of a three-dimensional figure or body: *the streamlined **contour** of the hybrid vehicle.* ***Profile*** denotes the outline of something viewed against a background and especially the outline of the human face in side view: *The police took a photograph of the mugger's **profile**.*

fragile

fragile, breakable, frangible, flimsy, brittle

These adjectives mean easily broken or damaged. ***Fragile*** applies to objects that are not made of strong or sturdy material and that require great care when handled: ***fragile** porcelain plates.* ***Breakable*** and ***frangible*** mean capable of being broken but do not necessarily imply inherent weakness: ***breakable** toys; **frangible** bullets designed to break apart on impact.* ***Flimsy*** refers to what is easily broken because of inferior materials or workmanship: *"**Flimsy** and loosely built structures collapsed like houses of cards under the terrific wrenching and shaking"* (Richard L. Humphrey). ***Brittle*** refers to inelasticity that makes something especially likely to fracture or snap when it is subjected to pressure: ***brittle** bones.*

frank

frank, candid, forthright, outspoken, straightforward, open

These adjectives mean revealing or disposed to reveal one's thoughts freely and honestly. ***Frank*** implies directness, sometimes to the point of bluntness: *"And yes, to be **frank**, the singing was atrocious"* (Eileen Pollack). ***Candid*** and ***forthright*** often suggest refusal to evade difficult or unpleasant issues: *"Save, save, oh save me from the **candid** friend!"* (George Canning); *"He wanted his countrymen to know the truth, and he was **forthright** about the challenges they faced"* (Sean Hannity). ***Outspoken*** usually implies bold lack of reserve: *"She is **outspoken** to the point of never holding back, on politics or much else"* (Joseph Epstein). ***Straightforward*** denotes directness of manner and expression: *"George was a **straightforward** soul. . . . 'See here!' he said. 'Are you engaged to anybody?'"* (Booth Tarkington). ***Open*** suggests freedom from all trace of reserve or secretiveness: *"I will be **open** and sincere with you"* (Joseph Addison).

frighten

frighten, scare, alarm, terrify, terrorize, startle, panic

These verbs mean to cause a person to experience fear. ***Frighten*** and the more informal *scare* are the most widely applicable: *"The Count's mysterious warning **frightened** me at the time"* (Bram Stoker); *We **scared** each other telling ghost* *stories before bed.* **Alarm** implies a state of fearful anxiety, often brought on suddenly: *The sight of the approaching shark **alarmed** the swimmers.* **Terrify** implies overwhelming, often paralyzing fear: *"It is the coming of death that **terrifies** me"* (Oscar Wilde). To **terrorize** is to strike fear into another, often for purposes of coercion: *"The decent citizen was **terrorized** into paying public blackmail"* (Arthur Conan Doyle). **Startle** suggests a momentary fright that may cause a sudden, involuntary movement of the body: *The clap of thunder **startled** us.* **Panic** implies sudden frantic fear that often impairs self-control and rationality: *The realistic radio drama **panicked** the listeners who tuned in after it had begun.*

futile

futile, barren, bootless, fruitless, ineffectual, pointless, unavailing, useless, vain

These adjectives mean producing no result or effect: *a **futile** effort; **barren** research; **bootless** entreaties; **fruitless** labors; **ineffectual** treatments; **pointless** comments; an **unavailing** attempt; a **useless** discussion; **vain** regrets.*
Antonym: **useful**

gather

gather, collect, assemble, congregate, accumulate, amass

These verbs mean to bring or come together in a group or aggregate. **Gather** is the most widely applicable: *I **gathered** sticks for the fire. Clouds **gathered** in the evening sky.* **Collect** frequently refers to the careful selection of like or related things that become part of an organized whole: *She **collects** stamps as a hobby.* In other contexts, **collect** suggests the gradual process by which similar items or materials come together to form a distinct mass: *Dust **collected** on the shelves. Leaves **collected** in the gutter.* **Assemble** implies a definite and usually close relationship. With respect to persons, the term suggests convening out of common interest or purpose: ***Assembling** an able staff was more difficult than expected. The reporters **assembled** for the press conference.* With respect to things, **assemble** implies gathering and fitting together components: *The curator is **assembling** an interesting exhibit of Stone Age artifacts.* **Congregate** refers chiefly to the coming together of a large number of persons or animals: *The students **congregated** after class to compare notes.* **Accumulate** applies to the increase of like or related things over an extended period: *They **accumulated** enough capital to invest. Old newspapers **accumulated** in the basement.* **Amass** refers to the collection or accumulation of things, often valuable things, to form an imposing quantity: *Their families had **amassed** great fortunes. Rocks had **amassed** at the bottom of the glacier.*

gaze

gaze, stare, gape, gawk, glare, peer

These verbs mean to look long and intently. **Gaze** is often indicative of wonder, fascination, awe, or admiration: ***gazing** at the stars; **gazing** into a lover's eyes.* **Stare** can indicate curiosity, boldness, rudeness, or stupidity: ***stared** closely at the creatures in the aquarium; warned the children not to **stare** at strangers.* **Gape** suggests a prolonged open-mouthed look reflecting amazement, awe, or lack of intelligence: *tourists **gaping** at the sights.* To **gawk** is to gape or stare foolishly or rudely: *Drivers **gawked** at the overturned truck.* To ***glare*** is to fix another with a hard, piercing stare: ***glared** furiously at me for giving away her secret.* To ***peer*** is to look narrowly, searchingly, and seemingly with difficulty: ***peered** at us through her glasses.*

ghastly

ghastly, gruesome, grisly, grim, macabre

These adjectives describe what is shockingly repellent in aspect or appearance. *Ghastly* suggests the shock or horror inspired by violent death or bodily harm: *the **ghastly** toll of trench warfare; a **ghastly** disfiguring disease.* *Gruesome* and *grisly* often describe what horrifies or revolts because of its graphic nature: *a **gruesome** murder scene; read about the **grisly** details of the accident.* *Grim* refers to what repels because of its harsh or unnerving nature: *the **grim** task of burying the earthquake victims.* *Macabre* can suggest the fascination as well as the horror of unnatural death and is often used of artistic works: *a murder mystery with a **macabre** twist at the end.*

glad

glad, happy, cheerful, lighthearted, joyful, joyous

These adjectives mean being in or showing good spirits. *Glad* often refers to the feeling that results from the gratification of a wish or from satisfaction with immediate circumstances: *"They were smiling, lifting their hands to me, **glad** to be together, **glad** to see me"* (Wendell Berry). *Happy* applies to a feeling of pleasure, satisfaction, or joy: *"Ask yourself whether you are **happy**, and you cease to be so"* (John Stuart Mill). *Cheerful* suggests characteristic good spirits: *a **cheerful** volunteer.* *Lighthearted* stresses the absence of care: *"We knew that things were hard for our Bohemian neighbors, but the two girls were **lighthearted** and never complained"* (Willa Cather). *Joyful* and *joyous* suggest lively, often exultant happiness: *a **joyful** heart; **joyous** laughter.*

grand

grand, magnificent, imposing, stately, majestic, august

These adjectives mean strikingly large in size, scope, or extent. Both *grand* and *magnificent* apply to what is physically or aesthetically impressive. *Grand* implies dignity, sweep, or eminence: *a **grand** hotel lobby with marble floors.* *Magnificent* suggests splendor, sumptuousness, and grandeur: *a **magnificent** cathedral.* *Imposing* describes what impresses by virtue of its size, bearing, or power: *an **imposing** array of skyscrapers.* *Stately* refers principally to what is dignified and handsome: *a **stately** home set back from the street.* *Majestic* suggests lofty dignity or sublime beauty: *the **majestic** snowcapped Alps.* *August* describes what inspires solemn reverence or awe: *the **august** presence of the black-robed judges.*

grieve

grieve, lament, mourn, sorrow

These verbs mean to feel, show, or express grief, sadness, or regret: ***grieved** over her father's death; **lamenting** about the decline in academic standards; **mourns** for lost hopes; **sorrowed** for a lost friend.*
Antonym: rejoice

gruff | **gruff, brusque, blunt, curt**

These adjectives mean abrupt and sometimes discourteous in manner or speech. *Gruff* implies roughness or surliness but does not necessarily suggest rudeness: *a decent fellow once you get past the **gruff** manner.* **Brusque** emphasizes rude abruptness: *dismissed us with a **brusque** wave of the hand.* **Blunt** stresses utter frankness and usually a disconcerting directness: *was **blunt** in her disapproval of the idea.* **Curt** denotes usually rude briefness and abruptness of speech: *a **curt**, two-line letter of rejection.*

guide | **guide, lead, pilot, shepherd, steer, usher**

These verbs mean to conduct on or direct to the way: ***guided** me to my seat; **led** the troops into battle; a teacher **piloting** students through the zoo; **shepherding** tourists to the bus; **steered** the applicant to the third floor; **ushering** a visitor out.*

habit | **habit, practice, custom, wont**

These nouns denote patterns of behavior established by continual repetition. *Habit* applies to a behavior or practice so ingrained that it is often done without conscious thought: *"**Habit** rules the unreflecting herd"* (William Wordsworth). *Practice* denotes an often chosen pattern of individual or group behavior: *"You will find it a very good **practice** always to verify your references, sir"* (Martin Joseph Routh). *Custom* is behavior as established by long practice and especially by accepted conventions: *"No written law has ever been more binding than unwritten **custom** supported by popular opinion"* (Carrie Chapman Catt). *Wont* refers to a customary and distinctive practice: *"Miss Roxy sat bolt upright, as was her **wont**"* (Harriet Beecher Stowe).

happen | **happen, befall, betide, chance, occur**

These verbs mean to come about: *saw an awful thing **happen**; predicted that misery will **befall** humankind; woe that **betides** the poor soldier; former friends who **chanced** to meet again; described the accident exactly as it **occurred**.*

harass | **harass, harry, hound, badger, pester, plague**

These verbs mean to trouble persistently or incessantly. *Harass* and *harry* imply systematic persecution by besieging with repeated annoyances, threats, or demands: *The landlord **harassed** the tenants who were behind in their rent.* *"John Adams and John Quincy Adams, pillars of personal rectitude, were **harried** throughout their presidencies by accusations of corruption, fraud, and abuses of power"* (Alan Brinkley and Davis Dyer). *Hound* suggests unrelenting pursuit to gain a desired end: *Reporters **hounded** the celebrity for an interview.* To *badger* is to nag or entreat persistently: *The child **badgered** his parents for a new bicycle.* To *pester* is to inflict a succession of petty annoyances: *"How she would have pursued and **pestered** me with questions and surmises"* (Charlotte Brontë). *Plague* refers to a problem likened to a noxious disease: *"As I have no estate, I am **plagued** with no tenants or stewards"* (Henry Fielding).

haste   **haste, celerity, dispatch, expedition, hurry, speed**

These nouns denote rapidity or promptness of movement or activity: *left the room in **haste**; a train moving with great **celerity**; advanced with all possible **dispatch**; finished the project with remarkable **expedition** so as to meet the deadline; was in a **hurry** to get home; driving with excessive **speed**.*
Antonym: **deliberation**

hateful   **hateful, detestable, odious, offensive, repellent**

These often interchangeable adjectives describe what elicits or deserves strong dislike, distaste, or revulsion. ***Hateful*** refers to what evokes hatred or deep animosity: *"No vice is universally so **hateful** as ingratitude"* (Joseph Priestley). ***Detestable*** applies to what arouses abhorrence or scorn: ***detestable** crimes against humanity*. Something ***odious*** is the object of intense displeasure or aversion: *"the **odious** practice of sending prisoners abroad to be tortured"* (Ronald Dworkin). ***Offensive*** applies to what offends or insults: *an **offensive** suggestion that the writer was guilty of plagiarism*. Something ***repellent*** arouses repugnance or disgust: *"[The motion picture code] banned the portrayal of **repellent** subjects—the sale of women, surgical operations, cruelty to children and animals"* (Jeffrey Meyers).

healthy   **healthy, wholesome, sound, hale, robust, well**

These adjectives refer to a state of good physical health. ***Healthy*** stresses the absence of disease or infirmity and is used of whole organisms as well as their parts: *a **healthy** baby; flossed daily to promote **healthy** gums*. ***Wholesome*** suggests a state of good health associated with youthful vitality or clean living: *"In truth, a **wholesome**, ruddy, blooming creature she was"* (Harriet Beecher Stowe). ***Healthy*** and ***wholesome*** are often extended to conditions or choices deemed conducive to good health: *a **healthy** lifestyle; **wholesome** foods*. ***Sound*** emphasizes freedom from injury, imperfection, or impairment: *"The man with the toothache thinks everyone happy whose teeth are **sound**"* (George Bernard Shaw). ***Hale*** stresses freedom from infirmity, especially in elderly persons, while ***robust*** emphasizes healthy strength and ruggedness: *"He is pretty well advanced in years, but hale, **robust**, and florid"* (Tobias Smollett). ***Well*** indicates absence of or recovery from illness: *felt **well** enough to make the trip*.

heap   **heap, mound, pile, stack**

These nouns denote a group or collection of things lying one on top of the other: *a **heap** of old newspapers; a **mound** of boulders; a **pile** of boxes; a **stack** of firewood*.

heavy   **heavy, weighty, hefty, massive, ponderous**

These adjectives mean having a relatively great weight. ***Heavy*** refers to what has great physical weight (*a **heavy** boulder*) and figuratively to what is burdensome or oppressive to the spirit (*heavy responsibilities*). *Weighty* literally denotes having considerable weight (*a weighty package*); figuratively, it describes what is onerous, serious, or important (*a weighty decision*). *Hefty* refers principally to physical heaviness or brawniness: *a hefty book; a short, hefty wrestler*. *Massive* describes what is bulky, heavy, solid, and strong: *massive marble columns*. *Ponderous* refers to what has great mass and weight and usually implies unwieldiness: *ponderous prehistoric beasts*. Figuratively it describes what is complicated, involved, or lacking in grace: *a book with a ponderous plot*.

heritage   heritage, inheritance, legacy, tradition

These nouns denote something immaterial, such as a practice or custom, that is passed from one generation to another: *a heritage of volunteerism; a rich inheritance of storytelling; a legacy of philosophical thought; the family tradition of going for a walk on Thanksgiving*.

hide   hide, conceal, secrete, cache, cloak

These verbs mean to keep from the sight or knowledge of others. *Hide* and *conceal* are the most general and are often used interchangeably: *I used a throw rug to hide (or conceal) the stain on the carpet. I smiled to hide (or conceal) my hurt feelings*. *Secrete* and *cache* involve concealment in a place unknown to others; *cache* often implies storage for later use: *The lioness secreted her cubs in the tall grass. The mountain climbers cached their provisions in a cave*. To *cloak* is to conceal something by masking or disguising it: *"On previously cloaked issues, the Soviets have suddenly become forthcoming"* (John McLaughlin).

hobble   hobble, fetter, handcuff, hogtie, manacle, shackle

These verbs mean to restrict the activity or free movement of: *a graduate hobbled by debt; researchers fettered by outmoded thinking; entrepreneurs handcuffed by rigid regulations; leadership that refused to be hogtied; imagination manacled by fear; an artist shackled by convention*.

idea   idea, thought, notion, concept, conception

These nouns refer to what is formed or represented in the mind as the product of mental activity. *Idea* has the widest range: *"Human history is in essence a history of ideas"* (H.G. Wells). *Thought* is distinctively intellectual and stresses contemplation and reasoning: *She gathered her thoughts before she spoke*. *Notion* suggests an often intuitive idea or image conceived by the mind: *"All that came to mind was a notion of galactic space, of spirals, the Horse Nebula, all of which were distant and mysterious and cold"* (Craig Nova). *Concept* and *conception* are applied to mental formulations on a broad scale: *You seem to have absolutely no concept of time. "Every succeeding scientific discovery makes greater nonsense of old-time conceptions of sovereignty"* (Anthony Eden).

ideal   ideal, exemplar, model, standard, pattern

These nouns refer to someone or something worthy of imitation or duplication. An ***ideal*** represents a sometimes unattainable level of perfection: *"Religion is the vision of . . . something which is the ultimate **ideal**, and the hopeless quest"* (Alfred North Whitehead). An ***exemplar***, like a ***model***, serves as a worthy example by being the best or most admirable of its class: *"He is indeed the perfect **exemplar** of all nobleness"* (Jane Porter); *"Our fellow countryman is a **model** of a man"* (Charles Dickens). A ***standard*** is a basis of comparison or judgment: *"Alexander's conquests created a legend that would provide the **standard** by which other leaders measured their careers"* (Eugene N. Borza). A ***pattern*** is an example worthy of imitation by reason of being an original or essential form of something: *"I will be the **pattern** of all patience"* (Shakespeare).

imbue   imbue, permeate, pervade, saturate, suffuse

These verbs mean to cause to be filled with a particular quality, such as an attitude or feeling: *poetry **imbued** with lyricism; optimism that **permeates** a group; letters **pervaded** with gloom; a play **saturated** with ironic witticism; a heart **suffused** with love.*

imitate   imitate, copy, mimic, ape, parody, simulate

These verbs mean to follow something or someone taken as a model. To ***imitate*** is to act like or follow a pattern or style set by another: *"The Blue Jay is . . . a renowned vocal mimic, with the uncanny ability to **imitate** hawk calls"* (Marie Read). To ***copy*** is to duplicate an original as precisely as possible: *"His grandfather had spent a laborious life-time in Rome, **copying** the Old Masters for a generation which lacked the facile resource of the camera"* (Edith Wharton). To ***mimic*** is to make a close imitation, often to ridicule: *"[He] **mimicked** the vacuum salesman as he explained his attachments, clearing his throat before each sentence, twisting the phantom hose"* (Deirdre McNamer). To ***ape*** is to follow another's lead, often with an absurd result: *"Those [superior] states of mind do not come from **aping** an alien culture"* (John Russell). To ***parody*** is either to imitate comically or to attempt a serious imitation and fail: *"All these peculiarities [of Samuel Johnson's literary style] have been imitated by his admirers and **parodied** by his assailants"* (Thomas Macaulay). To ***simulate*** is to replicate something's appearance or character: *"An ecological community can sometimes **simulate** the intricate harmony of a single organism"* (Richard Dawkins).

impetuous   impetuous, hasty, headlong, precipitate

These adjectives describe abruptness or lack of deliberation. ***Impetuous*** suggests forceful impulsiveness or impatience: *"[Martin Luther King] feared that an ill-prepared, **impetuous** demonstration would endanger . . . the marchers"* (Nick Kotz). ***Hasty*** and ***headlong*** both stress hurried, often reckless action: *"**Hasty** marriage seldom proveth well"* (Shakespeare). *"In his **headlong** flight down the circular staircase, . . . [he] had pitched forward violently . . . and probably broken*

his neck" (Mary Roberts Rinehart). ***Precipitate*** suggests impulsiveness and lack of due reflection: "*All my mistakes in life had flowed from that **precipitate** departure of mine*" (Philip Roth).

importance   importance, consequence, significance, import, weight

These nouns refer to the state or quality of being significant, influential, or worthy of note or esteem. *Importance* is the most general term: *the **importance** of a proper diet.* ***Consequence*** is especially applicable to persons or things of notable rank or position (*scholars of **consequence***) and to what is important because of its possible outcome, result, or effect (*tax laws of **consequence** to investors*). ***Significance*** and ***import*** refer to the quality of something that gives it special meaning or value: *an event of real **significance**; works of great social **import**.* ***Weight*** suggests seriousness or authority: "*The popular faction at Rome . . . was led by men of **weight***" (J.A. Froude).

inactive   inactive, idle, inert, dormant, latent, quiescent

These adjectives mean not involved in or disposed to movement or activity. ***Inactive*** indicates absence of activity: *retired but not **inactive**; an **inactive** factory.* ***Idle*** refers to persons who are not doing anything or are not busy: *employees who were **idle** because of the strike.* It also refers to what is not in use or operation: ***idle** machinery.* ***Inert*** describes things powerless to move themselves or to produce a desired effect; applied to persons, it implies lethargy or sluggishness, especially of mind or spirit: "*The Honorable Mrs. Jamieson . . . was fat and **inert**, and very much at the mercy of her old servants*" (Elizabeth C. Gaskell). ***Dormant*** refers to a state of suspended activity but often implies the possibility of renewal: ***dormant** feelings of affection.* What is ***latent*** is present but not evident: ***latent** ability.* ***Quiescent*** sometimes—but not always—suggests temporary inactivity: "*For a time, he* [the whale] *lay **quiescent**"* (Herman Melville).

include   include, comprise, comprehend, embrace, encompass

These verbs mean to take in or contain as part of something larger. ***Include*** often implies an incomplete listing: "*Through the process of amendment, interpretation and court decision I have finally been **included** in 'We, the people'*" (Barbara C. Jordan). ***Comprise*** usually implies that all of the components are stated: *The book **comprises** 15 chapters.* ***Comprehend**, **embrace**,* and ***encompass*** usually refer to the taking in of subordinate elements: *My field of study **comprehends** several disciplines. This theory **embraces** many facets of human behavior. The debate **encompassed** all points of view.*

increase   increase, expand, enlarge, augment, multiply

These verbs mean to make or become greater or larger. ***Increase*** sometimes suggests steady growth: *The president's economic program is designed to **increase** consumer confidence. The city's population **increased** during the last decade.* ***Expand*** applies especially to an increase in size, volume, or scope: *Visiting the botanical garden has **expanded** my interest in tropical plants. These plant fibers* *expand when water is plentiful. **Enlarge** often implies an increase in size, area, or extent, as by widening or broadening: The landowner **enlarged** her property by repeated purchases. The disease causes the kidneys to **enlarge**. **Augment** usually* applies to an increase that is already developed or well under way: *She **augmented** her collection of books each month. As the pressure **augments,** the volume of the steam decreases.* To ***multiply*** is to increase in number: *The Internet has **multiplied** the ways in which consumers can buy goods. The number of tourists visiting the town has **multiplied** since the highway opened.*

indicate

indicate, attest, bespeak, betoken

These verbs mean to give grounds for supposing or inferring the existence or presence of something: *a fever **indicating** illness; paintings that **attest** the artist's genius; disorder that **bespeaks** negligence; melting snows that **betoken** spring floods.*

indispensable

indispensable, critical, essential, necessary, requisite

These adjectives apply to something that cannot be dispensed with: *foods that are **indispensable** to good nutrition; education that is **critical** to success; funds **essential** to completing the project; the **necessary** tools for the job; lacking the **requisite** qualifications for the position.*

inquiry

inquiry, inquisition, investigation, probe

These nouns denote a quest for knowledge, data, or truth: *filed an **inquiry** about the lost shipment; an **inquisition** into their political activities; a criminal **investigation**; a **probe** into alleged police corruption.*

intelligent

intelligent, bright, brilliant, smart, intellectual

These adjectives mean having or showing mental keenness. ***Intelligent*** usually implies the ability to cope with new problems and to use the power of reasoning and inference effectively: *The company put its most **intelligent** engineers to work on rectifying the design flaw.* ***Bright*** implies quickness or ease in learning: *She was a **bright** student who was soon at the head of the class.* ***Brilliant*** suggests unusually impressive mental acuteness: *"The dullard's envy of **brilliant** men is always assuaged by the suspicion that they will come to a bad end"* (Max Beerbohm). ***Smart*** refers to quick intelligence and often a ready capability for taking care of one's own interests: *You were **smart** to buy your house when prices were low.* ***Intellectual*** implies the capacity to grasp difficult or abstract concepts: *The former professor was the more **intellectual** candidate.*

intention

intention, intent, purpose, goal, end, aim, object, objective

These nouns refer to what one plans to do or achieve. ***Intention*** simply signifies a course of action that one proposes to follow: *It is my **intention** to work for a year and then go back to school.* ***Intent*** more strongly implies deliberateness: *The executor complied with the testator's **intent**.* ***Purpose*** stresses the desired result of one's actions or efforts and often implies a sense of dedication: *The organization's*

purpose is to build affordable housing. A *goal* is something rewarding or fulfilling that inspires a sustained endeavor: *The college's goal was to raise sixty million dollars for a new library.* **End** suggests an ultimate or overriding goal: *The candidate wanted to win and pursued every means to achieve that end.* **Aim** stresses the direction one's efforts take in pursuit of something: *The aim of the legislation is to spur the development of renewable energy.* An *object* is a specific outcome or result on which one is focused: *The object of chess is to checkmate your opponent's king.* An *objective* is a goal that one is assigned or motivated to achieve: *The report outlines the committee's objectives.*

irrelevant

irrelevant, extraneous, immaterial, impertinent

These adjectives mean not pertinent to the subject under consideration: *ignored irrelevant comments during the discussion; a question extraneous to the topic of the presentation; an objection that was declared to be immaterial to the case; deleted the impertinent facts from the report.*
Antonym: relevant

isolate

isolate, insulate, seclude, segregate, sequester

These verbs mean to separate from others: *a mountain that isolated the village from larger towns; insulated herself from the chaos surrounding her; a celebrity who was secluded from public scrutiny; segregated the infectious patients in a special ward; sequestering a jury during its deliberations.*

join

join, combine, unite, link, connect

These verbs mean to fasten or affix or become fastened or affixed. *Join* applies to the physical contact or union of at least two separate things and to the coming together of persons, as into a group: *The children joined hands. The two groups joined together to support the bill. "Join the union, girls, and together say* Equal Pay for Equal Work" (Susan B. Anthony). *Combine* suggests the mixing or merging of components, often for a specific purpose: *The cook combined various ingredients. The schools combined to make more efficient use of resources.* **Unite** stresses the coherence or oneness of the persons or things joined: *The volunteers united to prevent their town from flooding. The strike united the oppressed workers.* **Link** and **connect** imply a firm attachment in which the individual components remain distinct: *The study linked the high crime rate to unemployment. The reporter connected the police chief to the scandal.*

joke

joke, witticism, quip, crack, wisecrack, gag

These nouns refer to something that is said or done in order to evoke laughter or amusement. *Joke* especially denotes an amusing story with a punch line at the end: *told jokes at the party.* A *witticism* is a witty, usually cleverly phrased remark: *a speech full of witticisms.* A *quip* is a clever, pointed, often sarcastic remark: *responded to the tough questions with quips.* **Crack** and **wisecrack** refer less formally to flippant or sarcastic retorts: *made a crack about my driving* *ability; punished for making **wisecracks** in class. **Gag** is principally applicable to a broadly comic remark or to comic by-play in a theatrical routine: one of the most memorable **gags** in the history of vaudeville.*

keep

keep, retain, withhold, reserve

These verbs mean to have and maintain in one's possession or control. ***Keep*** is the most general: *We received a few offers but decided to **keep** the house.* ***Retain*** means to continue to hold, especially in the face of possible loss: *Though unhappy, he **retained** his sense of humor.* ***Withhold*** implies reluctance or refusal to give, grant, or allow: *The tenant **withheld** his rent until the owner fixed the boiler.* To ***reserve*** is to hold back for the future or for a special purpose: *The farmer **reserved** two acres for an orchard.*

knowledge

knowledge, information, learning, erudition, scholarship, lore

These nouns refer to what is known, as through study or experience. ***Knowledge*** is the broadest: *"Science is organized **knowledge**"* (Herbert Spencer). ***Information*** often implies a collection of facts and data: *"A man's judgment cannot be better than the **information** on which he has based it"* (Arthur Hays Sulzberger). ***Learning*** usually refers to knowledge gained by schooling and study: *"**Learning** . . . must be sought for with ardor and attended to with diligence"* (Abigail Adams). ***Erudition*** implies profound, often specialized knowledge: *"Some have criticized his poetry as elitist, unnecessarily impervious to readers who do not share his **erudition**"* (Elizabeth Kastor). ***Scholarship*** is the mastery of a particular area of learning reflected in a scholar's work: *A good journal article shows ample evidence of the author's **scholarship**.* ***Lore*** is usually applied to knowledge gained through tradition or anecdote about a particular subject: *Many American folktales concern the **lore** of frontier life.*

laconic

laconic, reticent, taciturn, tightlipped

These adjectives describe people who are sparing with speech. ***Laconic*** denotes terseness or conciseness in expression, but when applied to people it often implies an unwillingness to use words: *"Mountain dwellers and mountain lovers are a **laconic** tribe. They know the futility of words"* (Edna Ferber). ***Reticent*** suggests a reluctance to share one's thoughts and feelings: *"She had been shy and **reticent** with me, and now . . . she was telling me aloud the secrets of her inmost heart"* (W.H. Hudson). ***Taciturn*** implies unsociableness and a tendency to speak only when it is absolutely necessary: *"At the Council board he was **taciturn**; and in the House of Lords he never opened his lips"* (Thomas Macaulay). ***Tightlipped*** strongly implies a steadfast unwillingness to divulge information being sought: *He remained **tightlipped** when asked about his personal life.*

large

large, big, great

These adjectives mean being notably above the average in size or magnitude: *a **large** sum of money; a **big** red barn; a **great** ocean liner.*
Antonym: small

last

last, final, terminal, ultimate

These adjectives mean coming after all others in chronology or sequence. *Last* applies to what comes at the end of a series: *the **last** day of the month*. Something *final* stresses the definitiveness and decisiveness of the conclusion: *Somehow he always seems to get the **final** word in what we end up doing.* *Terminal* applies to what marks or forms a limit or boundary, as in space, time, or development: *That railroad's **terminal** city is a town with a large harbor.* *Ultimate* applies to what concludes a series, process, or progression or constitutes a final result or objective: *the **ultimate** sonata of that opus; our **ultimate** goal; the **ultimate** effect.*

lean

lean, skinny, scrawny, lank, lanky, gaunt

These adjectives mean lacking excess flesh. *Lean* emphasizes absence of fat but usually suggests good health: *fattened the **lean** cattle for market.* *Skinny* and *scrawny* imply unattractive thinness, as from undernourishment: *The child has **skinny** legs with prominent knees. "He [had] a long, **scrawny** neck that rose out of a very low collar"* (Winston Churchill). *Lank* describes one who is thin and tall, and *lanky* one who is thin, tall, and ungraceful: *"He was . . . exceedingly **lank**, with narrow shoulders"* (Washington Irving). *The boy had developed into a **lanky** adolescent.* *Gaunt* implies boniness and a haggard appearance; it may suggest illness or hardship: *a white-haired pioneer, her face **gaunt** from overwork.*

lethargy

lethargy, lassitude, torpor, languor

These nouns refer to a deficiency in mental and physical alertness and activity. *Lethargy* is a state of sluggishness, drowsy dullness, or apathy: *"Your **lethargy** is such that you will not fight even to protect the freedom which your mothers won for you"* (Virginia Woolf). *Lassitude* implies weariness or diminished energy such as might result from physical or mental strain: *"His anger had evaporated; he felt nothing but utter **lassitude**"* (John Galsworthy). *Torpor* suggests the suspension of activity characteristic of an animal in hibernation: *"Confinement induced **torpor**, and from **torpor** he could easily slip to passivity, resignation, death"* (Larry McMurtry). *Languor* is the indolence typical of one who is satiated by a life of luxury or pleasure: *"with that slow, catlike way about him, cool, aloof, almost contemptuous in the **languor** and ease of his movements"* (Tobias Wolff).

level

level, flat, even, plane, smooth, flush

These adjectives describe surfaces without elevations or depressions. *Level* implies being parallel with the line of the horizon: *acres of **level** farmland.* *Flat* applies to surfaces without curves, protuberances, or indentations: *a **flat** rock.* *Even* refers to flat surfaces in which no part is higher or lower than another: *the **even** surface of the mirror.* *Plane* is a mathematical term referring to a surface containing all the straight lines connecting any two points on it: *a **plane** figure.* *Smooth* describes a surface on which the absence of irregularities can be established by sight or touch: **smooth** *marble*. **Flush** applies to a surface that is on an exact level with an adjoining one: *a door that is* **flush** *with the wall*.

liberal   liberal, freehanded, generous, munificent, openhanded

These adjectives mean willing or marked by a willingness to give unstintingly: *a* **liberal** *backer of the arts; a* **freehanded** *host; a* **generous** *donation; a* **munificent** *gift; fond and* **openhanded** *grandparents*.
Antonym: stingy

mercy   mercy, leniency, clemency, charity

These nouns mean humane and kind, sympathetic, or forgiving treatment of or disposition toward others. **Mercy** is compassionate forbearance: *"The challenge . . . is how to define morally reasonable grounds on which to grant perpetrators* **mercy** *and allow them to go free"* (Pumla Gobodo-Madikizela). **Leniency** implies mildness, gentleness, and often a tendency to reduce punishment: *"Even though Grant advocated* **leniency** *toward the Confederacy's military leaders, he called for punishment of its political leaders"* (Brooks D. Simpson). **Clemency** is mercy shown by someone with judicial authority: *The judge believed in* **clemency** *for youthful offenders*. **Charity** is goodwill and benevolence in judging others: *"With malice toward none, with* **charity** *for all . . . let us strive on to finish the work we are in"* (Abraham Lincoln).

mix   mix, blend, mingle, merge, amalgamate, coalesce, fuse

These verbs mean to put into or come together in one mass so that constituent parts or elements are diffused or commingled. **Mix** is the least specific: *The cook* **mixed** *eggs, flour, and sugar. Do work and play never* **mix***?* To **blend** is to mix intimately and harmoniously so that the components lose their original definition: *The clerk* **blended** *mocha and java coffee beans. Snow-covered mountains* **blended** *into the clouds*. **Mingle** implies combination without loss of individual characteristics: *"Respect was* **mingled** *with surprise"* (Sir Walter Scott); *"His companions* **mingled** *freely and joyously with the natives"* (Washington Irving). **Merge** and **amalgamate** imply resultant homogeneity: *Tradition and innovation are* **merged** *in this new composition. Twilight* **merged** *into night. "The four sentences of the original are* **amalgamated** *into two"* (William Minto). **Coalesce** implies a slow merging: *Indigenous peoples and conquerors* **coalesced** *into the present-day population*. **Fuse** emphasizes an enduring union, as that formed by heating metals: *"He diffuses a tone and spirit of unity, that blends, and (as it were)* **fuses***, each into each"* (Samuel Taylor Coleridge).

moment   moment, instant, minute, second, jiffy, flash

These nouns denote a brief interval of time. A **moment** is an indeterminately short but significant period: *I'll be with you in a* **moment***. **Instant** is a period of time almost too brief to detect; it implies haste: *He hesitated for just an* **instant***. **Minute** is often interchangeable with **moment** and **second** with **instant**: *The alarm will ring any* **minute***. I'll be back in a* **second***. **Jiffy** and **flash** are somewhat informal and usually combine with *in a*; *in a jiffy* means in a short space of time, while *in a flash* suggests the almost imperceptible duration of a flash of light: *He went to the store but will be back in a jiffy. She finished the job in a flash.*

moral

moral, ethical, virtuous, righteous

These adjectives mean in accord with right or good conduct. *Moral* applies to personal character and behavior: *"Our moral sense dictates a clearcut preference for these societies which share with us an abiding respect for individual human rights"* (Jimmy Carter). *Ethical* stresses idealistic standards of right and wrong: *"Ours is a world of nuclear giants and ethical infants"* (Omar Bradley). *Virtuous* implies moral excellence and loftiness of character: *"The life of the nation is secure only while the nation is honest, truthful, and virtuous"* (Frederick Douglass). *Righteous* emphasizes moral uprightness; when it is applied to actions, reactions, or impulses, it often implies justifiable outrage: *"It was righteous anger that motivated letters written by whistle-blowing employees"* (Sandra P. Thomas).

move

move, affect, touch

These verbs mean to stir the emotions of a person or group. *Move* suggests a strong or deep emotional impact that is often expressed openly: *a performer who moved the audience to laughter and tears; scenes of famine that moved us to pity. Affect* can suggest a quieter but more persistent emotional state, as of grief, awe, or sorrow: *"Roosevelt was deeply affected by his loss. One by one, the President's closest companions had fallen away"* (Geoffrey C. Ward). *Touch* implies a personal and often inspirational experience, as of sympathy, admiration, or tenderness: *"Mr. Micawber pressed my hand, and groaned, and afterwards shed tears. I was greatly touched"* (Charles Dickens).

moving

moving, stirring, poignant, touching, affecting

These adjectives mean arousing or capable of arousing deep, usually somber emotion. *Moving* is the least specific: *"A . . . widow . . . has laid her case of destitution before him, in a very moving letter"* (Nathaniel Hawthorne). Something *stirring* excites strong, turbulent, but not unpleasant feelings: *a stirring speech about patriotism. Poignant* suggests the evocation of keen, painful emotion: *"The happier our new relations seemed, the stronger I felt an undercurrent of poignant sadness"* (Vladimir Nabokov). *Touching* emphasizes sympathy or tenderness: *a touching eulogy. Affecting* applies especially to what is heart-rending or bittersweet: *We found the photo of the hostages' release to be deeply affecting.*

muscular

muscular, brawny, burly, sinewy

These adjectives mean strong and powerfully built: *a muscular build; brawny arms; a burly stevedore; a lean and sinewy frame.*

mysterious   mysterious, esoteric, arcane, occult, cryptic, enigmatic

These adjectives mean beyond human power to explain or understand. Something *mysterious* arouses wonder and inquisitiveness: *"The sea lies all about us. . . . In its **mysterious** past it encompasses all the dim origins of life"* (Rachel Carson). What is *esoteric* is mysterious because only a select group knows and understands it: *a compilation of **esoteric** philosophical essays.* *Arcane* applies to what is hidden from general knowledge: ***arcane** economic theories.* *Occult* suggests knowledge reputedly gained only by secret, magical, or supernatural means: *an **occult** rite.* *Cryptic* suggests a sometimes deliberately puzzling terseness: *His roommate left **cryptic** messages alluding to his whereabouts.* Something *enigmatic* is mysterious and puzzling: *The biography struggles to make sense of the artist's **enigmatic** life.*

naive   naive, simple, ingenuous, unsophisticated, natural, unaffected, guileless, artless

These adjectives mean free from guile, cunning, or sham. *Naive* sometimes connotes a credulity that impedes effective functioning in a practical world: *"this **naive** simple creature, with his straightforward and friendly eyes so eager to believe appearances"* (Arnold Bennett). *Simple* stresses absence of complexity, artifice, pretentiousness, or dissimulation: *"Those of highest worth and breeding are most **simple** in manner and attire"* (Francis Parkman); *"Among **simple** people she had the reputation of being a prodigy of information"* (Harriet Beecher Stowe). *Ingenuous* denotes childlike directness, simplicity, and innocence; it connotes an inability to mask one's feelings: *an **ingenuous** admission of responsibility.* *Unsophisticated* indicates absence of worldliness: *the astonishment of **unsophisticated** tourists at the tall buildings.* *Natural* stresses spontaneity that is the result of freedom from self-consciousness or inhibitions: *"When Kavanagh was present, Alice was happy, but embarrassed; Cecilia, joyous and **natural**"* (Henry Wadsworth Longfellow). *Unaffected* implies sincerity and lack of affectation: *"With men he can be rational and **unaffected**, but when he has ladies to please, every feature works"* (Jane Austen). *Guileless* signifies absence of insidious or treacherous cunning: *a **guileless**, disarming look.* *Artless* stresses absence of plan or purpose and suggests unconcern for or lack of awareness of the reaction produced in others: *a child of **artless** grace and simple goodness.*

negligent   negligent, derelict, lax, neglectful, remiss, slack

These adjectives mean guilty of a lack of due care or concern: *The **negligent** landlord failed to repair the window.* *By not voting, he was **derelict** in his civic duty.* *If you're **lax** in attending class, your grades will suffer.* *Many neighbors felt that he had been **neglectful** of his property.* *It was **remiss** of her not to call to tell us she was coming.* *The teacher was **slack** in maintaining discipline.*

new | **new, fresh, novel, original**

These adjectives describe what has existed for only a short time, has only lately come into use, or has only recently arrived at a state or position, as of prominence: *New* is the most general: *a **new** movie; a **new** friend; a **new** opportunity.* Something *fresh* has qualities of newness such as briskness, brightness, or purity: ***fresh** footprints in the snow; **fresh** hope of discovering a vaccine.* **Novel** applies to the new and strikingly unusual: *"His sermons were considered bold in thought and **novel** in language"* (Edith Wharton). Something that is **original** is novel and the first of its kind: *"The science of pure mathematics, in its modern development, may claim to be the most **original** creation of the human spirit"* (Alfred North Whitehead).

noise | **noise, din, racket, uproar, pandemonium, hullabaloo, hubbub, clamor**

These nouns refer to loud, confused, or disagreeable sound or sounds. ***Noise*** is the least specific: *deafened by the **noise** in the subway.* A ***din*** is a jumble of loud, usually discordant sounds: *the **din** of the factory.* ***Racket*** is loud, distressing noise: *the **racket** made by trucks rolling along cobblestone streets.* ***Uproar, pandemonium,*** and ***hullabaloo*** imply disorderly tumult together with loud, bewildering sound: *"The evening **uproar** of the howling monkeys burst out"* (W.H. Hudson); *"a **pandemonium** of dancing and whooping, drumming and feasting"* (Francis Parkman); *a tremendous **hullabaloo** in the agitated crowd.* ***Hubbub*** emphasizes turbulent activity and concomitant din: *the **hubbub** of bettors, speculators, and tipsters.* ***Clamor*** is loud, usually sustained noise, as of a public outcry of dissatisfaction: *"not in the **clamor** of the crowded street"* (Henry Wadsworth Longfellow); *a debate that was interrupted by a **clamor** of opposition.*

noticeable | **noticeable, marked, conspicuous, prominent, salient, striking**

These adjectives mean tending to attract notice. ***Noticeable*** refers to something that can be readily noticed or observed: *The player's great height provided a very **noticeable** advantage on the basketball court.* What is ***marked*** is emphatically evident: *a **marked** limp; a **marked** success.* ***Conspicuous*** applies to what is immediately apparent and noteworthy: *a shirt with a **conspicuous** stain; a leader occupying a **conspicuous** place in the nation's history.* ***Prominent*** connotes a standing out, especially from others of a kind: *a **prominent** landmark; **prominent** moments in her career.* What is ***salient*** is so prominent and consequential that it seems to leap out and claim the attention: *His most **salient** feature is his irrepressible sense of humor.* ***Striking*** describes something that seizes the attention and produces a vivid impression on the sight or the mind: *The child bears a **striking** resemblance to his uncle.*

observe | **observe, keep, celebrate, commemorate, solemnize**

These verbs mean to give proper heed to or show proper reverence for something, such as a custom or holiday. *Observe* and *keep* stress compliance or respectful adherence to that which is prescribed: *observes the Sabbath;* *keeps the holiday traditions.* *Celebrate* emphasizes observance in the form of rejoicing or festivity: *a surprise party to* *celebrate* *her birthday.* To *commemorate* is to honor the memory of a past event: *a ceremony that* *commemorated* *the career of a physician.* *Solemnize* implies dignity and gravity in the celebration of an occasion: *solemnized the funeral with a 21-gun salute.*

obstinate   obstinate, stubborn, headstrong, recalcitrant, intractable, bullheaded, pigheaded, mulish

These adjectives mean tenaciously unwilling to yield. *Obstinate* implies unreasonable rigidity: *"Mr. Quincy labored hard with the governor to obtain his assent, but he was* *obstinate"* (Benjamin Franklin). *Stubborn* pertains to innate, often perverse resoluteness or unyieldingness: *"She was very* *stubborn* *when her mind was made up"* (Samuel Butler). One who is *headstrong* is obstinately bent on having his or her own way: *The* *headstrong* *senator ignored his constituency.* A person who is *recalcitrant* rebels against authority: *The police arrested the* *recalcitrant* *protestors.* *Intractable* refers to what is obstinate and difficult to manage or control: *"the* *intractable* *ferocity of his captive"* (Edgar Allan Poe). *Bullheaded* suggests foolish or irrational obstinacy, and *pigheaded,* stupid obstinacy: *Don't be* *bullheaded; see a doctor.* *"It's a pity pious folks are so apt to be* *pigheaded"* (Harriet Beecher Stowe). *Mulish* implies the obstinacy and intractability associated with a mule: *"Obstinate is no word for it, for she is* *mulish"* (Ouida).

occurrence   occurrence, happening, event, incident, episode

These nouns refer to something that takes place or comes to pass. *Occurrence* and *happening* are the most general: *an everyday* *occurrence; a* *happening* *of no great importance.* *Event* usually signifies a notable occurrence: *world* *events* *reported on the evening news.* *"Great* *events* *make me quiet and calm; it is only trifles that irritate my nerves"* (Victoria). *Incident* may apply to a minor occurrence: *an* *incident* *that was blown out of proportion in the press.* The term may also refer to a distinct event of sharp identity and significance: *an* *incident* *that changed scientists' understanding of the phenomenon.* An *episode* is an incident in the course of a progression or within a larger sequence: *"Happiness was but the occasional* *episode* *in a general drama of pain"* (Thomas Hardy).

offend   offend, insult, affront, outrage

These verbs mean to cause resentment, humiliation, or hurt. To *offend* is to cause displeasure, wounded feelings, or repugnance in another: *"He often* *offended* *men who might have been useful friends"* (John Lothrop Motley). *Insult* implies gross insensitivity, insolence, or contemptuous rudeness: *"My father had* *insulted* *her by refusing to come to our wedding"* (James Carroll). To *affront* is to insult openly, usually intentionally: *"He continued to belabor the poor woman in a studied effort to* *affront* *his hated chieftain"* (Edgar Rice Burroughs). *Outrage*

implies the flagrant violation of a person's integrity, pride, or sense of right and decency: "*He revered the men and women who transformed this piece of grassland into a great city, and he was **outraged** by the attacks on their reputation*" (James S. Hirsch).

offensive   offensive, disgusting, loathsome, nasty, odious, repellent, repulsive, revolting, vile

These adjectives mean extremely unpleasant to the senses or feelings: *an **offensive** remark; **disgusting** language; a **loathsome** disease; a **nasty** smell; an **odious** sight; a **repellent** demand; **repulsive** behavior; **revolting** food; **vile** thoughts.*

old   old, ancient, archaic, antediluvian, antique, antiquated

These adjectives describe what belongs to or dates from an earlier time or period. ***Old*** is the most general term: ***old** lace; an **old** saying.* ***Ancient*** pertains to the distant past: "*the hills, / Rock-ribbed, and **ancient** as the sun*" (William Cullen Bryant). ***Archaic*** implies a very remote, often primitive period: *an **archaic** Greek bronze of the seventh century* BC. ***Antediluvian*** applies to what is extremely outdated: "*I . . . went out to reconnoiter a fresh typewriter ribbon for Professor Mitwisser's **antediluvian** machine*" (Cynthia Ozick). ***Antique*** is applied to what is especially appreciated or valued because of its age: ***antique** furniture; an **antique** vase.* ***Antiquated*** describes what is out of date, no longer fashionable, or discredited: "*No idea is so **antiquated** that it was not once modern. No idea is so modern that it will not someday be **antiquated**"* (Ellen Glasgow).

opportunity   opportunity, occasion, opening, chance, break

These nouns refer to a favorable or advantageous circumstance or combination of circumstances. ***Opportunity*** is a favorable state of affairs or a suitable time: "*If you prepare yourself . . . you will be able to grasp **opportunity** for broader experience when it appears*" (Eleanor Roosevelt). ***Occasion*** suggests the proper time for an action or purpose: "*The celebration of the New Year is an **occasion** for optimism and hope*" (Bill Clinton). An ***opening*** is an opportunity affording a good possibility of success: *She waited patiently for her **opening**, then proved she was ready to lead the group.* ***Chance*** often implies an opportunity that arises through luck or accident: *Meeting each other at the coffee shop was a **chance** for us to chat.* A ***break*** is an often sudden piece of luck, especially good luck: *The aspiring actor got his first big **break** in Hollywood.*

oppose   oppose, fight, combat, resist, contest

These verbs mean to try to thwart or defeat someone or prevent or nullify something. ***Oppose*** has the widest application: ***opposed** the building of a nuclear power plant.* "*The idea is inconsistent with our constitutional theory and has been stubbornly **opposed** . . . since the early days of the Republic*" (E.B. White). ***Fight*** and ***combat*** suggest vigor and aggressiveness: "*All my life I have **fought** against prejudice and intolerance*" (Harry S. Truman); "*We are not afraid . . . to tolerate any error so long as reason is left free to **combat** it*" (Thomas Jefferson). To ***resist*** is to strive to fend off or offset the actions, effects, or force of: *"Pardon was freely extended to all who had **resisted** the invasion"* (John R. Green). To **contest** is to call something into question and take an active stand against it: ***contested*** *her neighbor's claims to her property in court.*

origin   origin, inception, source, root

These nouns signify the point at which something originates. ***Origin*** is the point at which something comes into existence: *The **origins** of some words are unknown.* When ***origin*** refers to people, it means parentage or ancestry: *"He came . . . of mixed French and Scottish **origin**"* (Charlotte Brontë). ***Inception*** is the beginning, as of an action or process: *The researcher was involved in the project from its **inception**. **Source** signifies the point at which something springs into being or from which it derives or is obtained: "The mysterious . . . is the **source** of all true art and science"* (Albert Einstein). ***Root*** often denotes what is considered the fundamental cause of or basic reason for something: *"Lack of money is the **root** of all evil"* (George Bernard Shaw).

outline   outline, contour, profile, silhouette

These nouns refer to a line that defines the boundary and shape of an object, mass, or figure: *the **outline** of the mountains against the sunset; saw the island's **contour** from the airplane; a monarch's **profile** on an ancient coin; saw the dark **silhouette** of the family waving farewell.*

pacify   pacify, mollify, conciliate, appease, placate, propitiate

These verbs refer to allaying another's anger, discontent, or agitation. To ***pacify*** is to ease the concerns of or restore calm to: *"The explanation . . . was merely an invention framed to **pacify** his guests"* (Charlotte Brontë). ***Mollify*** stresses the soothing of hostile feelings: *The therapist **mollified** the angry teenager by speaking gently. **Conciliate** implies winning over, often by reasoning and with mutual concessions: "He recognized the need to **conciliate** his political opponents"* (Robert W. Johannsen). ***Appease*** and ***placate*** suggest satisfying claims or demands or tempering antagonism, often by granting concessions: *I **appeased** my friend's anger with a compliment. A sincere apology **placated** the indignant customer. **Propitiate** often applies to an offended deity or an angry or powerful person: "All watch him . . . all laugh at his jokes, all seek to **propitiate** him"* (Charles Dickens).

partner   partner, colleague, ally, confederate

These nouns all denote one who is united or associated with another, as in a venture or relationship. A ***partner*** participates in a relationship in which each member has equal status: *a **partner** in a law firm.* A ***colleague*** is an associate in an occupation or a profession: *a **colleague** and fellow professor.* An ***ally*** is one who associates with another, at least temporarily, in a common cause: *countries that were **allies** in World War II.* A ***confederate*** is a member of a confederacy, league, or alliance or sometimes a collaborator in a suspicious venture: ***confederates*** *in a scheme to oust the chairman.*

passion | **passion, fervor, fire, zeal, ardor**

These nouns denote powerful, intense emotion. *Passion* is a deep, overwhelming emotion: "*There is not a passion so strongly rooted in the human heart as envy*" (Richard Brinsley Sheridan). The term may signify sexual desire or anger: "*He flew into a violent passion and abused me mercilessly*" (H.G. Wells). *Fervor* is great warmth and intensity of feeling: "*The union of the mathematician with the poet, fervor with measure, passion with correctness, this surely is the ideal*" (William James). *Fire* is burning passion: "*In our youth our hearts were touched with fire*" (Oliver Wendell Holmes, Jr.). *Zeal* is strong, enthusiastic devotion to a cause, ideal, or goal and tireless diligence in its furtherance: "*Laurie [resolved], with a glow of philanthropic zeal, to found and endow an institution for . . . women with artistic tendencies*" (Louisa May Alcott). *Ardor* is fiery intensity of feeling: "*When . . . Moby Dick was fairly sighted from the mast-heads, Macey, the chief mate, burned with ardor to encounter him*" (Herman Melville).

pause | **pause, intermission, recess, respite, suspension**

These nouns denote a temporary stop, as in activity: *a short pause in the conversation; a concert with a 15-minute intermission; the legislature's summer recess; toiling without respite; a suspension of work.*

perfect | **perfect, consummate, faultless, flawless, impeccable**

These adjectives mean being wholly without flaw: *a perfect diamond; a consummate performer; faultless logic; a flawless instrumental technique; speaks impeccable French.*

perform | **perform, execute, accomplish, achieve**

These verbs signify to carry through to completion. To *perform* is to carry out an action, undertaking, or procedure, often with great skill or care. *The ship's captain performed the wedding ceremony. Laser experiments are performed regularly in the laboratory. Execute* implies performing a task or putting something into effect in accordance with a plan or design: "*To execute laws is a royal office; to execute orders is not to be a king*" (Edmund Burke). *Accomplish* connotes the successful completion of something, often of something that requires tenacity or talent: "*Make one brave push and see what can be accomplished in a week*" (Robert Louis Stevenson). To *achieve* is to accomplish something, often something significant, especially despite difficulty: "*Some are born great . . . Some achieve greatness . . . And some have greatness thrust upon them*" (Shakespeare).

perplex | **perplex, mystify, bewilder, confound, puzzle**

These verbs mean to cause bafflement or confusion. *Perplex* stresses uncertainty or anxiety, as over reaching an understanding or finding a solution: "*No subject at the Philadelphia convention had perplexed the delegates more than the mode of choosing the president*" (Susan Dunn). *Mystify* implies something inexplicable by conventional understanding: "*Galileo was mystified by the disappearance of the two smaller bodies accompanying Saturn along its orbit*" (Eric Burgess). *Bewilder* emphasizes extreme mental confusion: "*We human beings are . . . **bewildered** when trying to imagine a world with more than three dimensions*" (Paul Davies). To **confound** is to confuse and astonish: *God hath chosen the foolish things of the world to **confound** the wise* (I Corinthians 1:27). ***Puzzle*** suggests difficulty in solving or interpreting something: "*The poor creature **puzzled** me once . . . by a question merely natural and innocent*" (Daniel Defoe).

pity   **pity, compassion, sympathy, empathy, commiseration, condolence**

These nouns signify kindly concern aroused by the misfortune, affliction, or suffering of another. ***Pity*** often implies a feeling of sorrow that inclines one to help or to show mercy. The word usually suggests that the person feeling pity is better off or in a superior position to the person who is the object of pity: "*Going with her mother everywhere, she saw what Althea did not: how the other women invited her out of **pity***" (Kate Wheeler). ***Compassion*** denotes deep awareness of the suffering of another and the wish to relieve it: "***Compassion** is not weakness, and concern for the unfortunate is not socialism*" (Hubert H. Humphrey). ***Sympathy*** denotes the act of or capacity for sharing in the sorrows or troubles of another: "*They had little **sympathy** to spare for their unfortunate enemies*" (William Hickling Prescott). ***Empathy*** is an identification with and understanding of another's situation, feelings, and motives: *Having changed schools several times as a child, I feel **empathy** for the transfer students.* ***Commiseration*** often entails the expression of pity or sorrow: *expressed their **commiseration** over the failure of the experiment.* ***Condolence*** is formal, conventional sympathy, usually toward a person who has experienced the loss of a loved one: *sent a letter of **condolence** to the bereaved family.*

plentiful   **plentiful, abundant, ample, copious, plenteous**

These adjectives mean being fully as much as one needs or desires: *a **plentiful** supply; the artist's **abundant** talent; **ample** space; **copious** provisions; a **plenteous** crop of wheat.*
Antonym: scant

praise   **praise, acclaim, commend, extol, laud**

These verbs mean to express approval or admiration. To **praise** is to voice approbation, commendation, or esteem: "*She was enthusiastically **praising** the beauties of Gothic architecture*" (Francis Marion Crawford). ***Acclaim*** usually implies hearty approbation warmly and publicly expressed: *The film was highly **acclaimed** by many critics.* ***Commend*** suggests moderate or restrained approval, as that accorded by a superior: *The judge **commended** the jury for their hard work.* ***Extol*** suggests exaltation or glorification: "*that sign of old age, **extolling** the past at the expense of the present*" (Sydney Smith). ***Laud*** connotes respectful or lofty praise: "*Comtosook was **lauded** as the most picture-perfect hamlet in the state*" (Jodi Picoult).

predicament   predicament, plight, quandary, jam, fix, pickle

These nouns refer to a difficult situation that has no readily discernible resolution or way out. A *predicament* is a problematic situation about which one does not know what to do: "*The wrenching predicament for conservation biologists is that endangered species reach the point of no return before their numbers fall to zero*" (Cynthia Mills). A *plight* is a bad or unfortunate situation: "*the plight of many single women in a society in which marriage tends to be regarded as the ideal state for a woman*" (Jane Wheare). A *quandary* is a state of perplexity, especially about what course of action to take: "*Having captured our men, we were in a quandary how to keep them*" (Theodore Roosevelt). The words *jam* and *fix* are more informal and refer to a predicament from which escape is difficult: "*The only way to be certain he will not get into some sort of a jam is to put a chain around his neck and lead him around like a performing bear*" (Jack Dempsey); "*Here was one murder defendant . . . who did not like to joke about the fix he was in*" (Robert Traver). Another informal term, a *pickle* is a disagreeable, embarrassing, or troublesome predicament: "*I could see no way out of the pickle I was in*" (Robert Louis Stevenson).

prevent   prevent, preclude, avert, obviate, forestall

These verbs mean to stop or hinder something from happening, especially by advance planning or action. *Prevent* implies anticipatory counteraction: "*Some contemporaries believed that capitalism and the rise of an international economy would prevent war among 'civilized' states*" (John Howard Morrow). To *preclude* is to exclude the possibility of an event or action: "*a tranquillity which . . . his wife's presence would have precluded*" (John Henry Newman). *Avert* and *obviate* imply that something, such as a difficulty or necessity, has been removed or avoided: *The pilot's quick thinking averted an accident. The short duration of the journey obviated the need for large food supplies. Forestall* usually suggests anticipatory measures taken to counteract, neutralize, or nullify the effects of something: *We installed an alarm system to forestall break-ins.*

produce   produce, bear, yield

These verbs mean to bring forth as a product: *a mine that produces gold; a seed that finally bore fruit; a plant that yields a medicinal oil.*

proficient   proficient, adept, skilled, skillful, accomplished, expert

These adjectives mean having or showing knowledge, ability, or skill, as in a profession or field of study. *Proficient* implies an advanced degree of competence acquired through training: *is proficient in Greek and Latin. Adept* suggests a natural aptitude improved by practice: *became adept at cutting the fabric without using a pattern. Skilled* implies sound, thorough competence and often mastery, as in an art, craft, or trade: *a skilled gymnast who won an Olympic medal.*

Skillful adds to *skilled* the idea of natural dexterity in performance or achievement: *is **skillful** in the use of the hand loom*. ***Accomplished*** bears with it a sense of refinement after much training and practice: *an **accomplished** violinist who played the sonata flawlessly*. ***Expert*** applies to one with consummate skill and command: *an **expert** negotiator who struck a deal between disputing factions*.

provoke   provoke, incite, excite, stimulate, arouse, rouse, stir

These verbs mean to move a person to action or feeling or to summon something into being by so moving a person. ***Provoke*** often merely states the consequences produced: *"Let my presumption not **provoke** thy wrath"* (Shakespeare); *"a situation which in the country would have **provoked** meetings"* (John Galsworthy). To ***incite*** is to provoke and urge on: *Members of the opposition **incited** the insurrection*. ***Excite*** implies a strong or emotional reaction: *The movie will fail—the plot **excites** little interest or curiosity*. ***Stimulate*** suggests renewed vigor of action as if by spurring or goading: *"Our vigilance was **stimulated** by our finding traces of a large . . . encampment"* (Francis Parkman). To ***arouse*** means to awaken, as from inactivity or apathy; ***rouse*** means the same, but more strongly implies vigorous or emotional excitement: *"In a democratic society like ours, relief must come through an **aroused** popular conscience that sears the conscience of the people's representatives"* (Felix Frankfurter); *"The oceangoing steamers . . . **roused** in him wild and painful longings"* (Arnold Bennett). To ***stir*** is to cause activity, strong but usually agreeable feelings, trouble, or commotion: *"It was him as **stirred** up th' young woman to preach last night"* (George Eliot); *"I have seldom been so . . . **stirred** by any piece of writing"* (Mark Twain).

push   push, propel, shove, thrust

These verbs mean to press against something in order to move it forward or aside: ***push** a baby carriage; wind **propelling** a sailboat; **shove** a tray across a table; **thrust** the package into her hand*.
Antonym: pull

quality   quality, property, attribute, character, trait

These nouns signify a feature that distinguishes or identifies someone or something: *explained the **qualities** of noble gases; tested the resilient **property** of rubber; knew the **attributes** of a fine wine; liked the rural **character** of the ranch; had positive **traits** such as kindness and generosity*.

quibble   quibble, carp, cavil, nitpick

These verbs mean to raise petty or frivolous objections or complaints: ***quibbling** about minor details; a critic who constantly **carped**; **caviling** about the price of coffee; tried to stop **nitpicking** all the time*.

range   **range, ambit, compass, orbit, purview, reach, scope, sweep**

These nouns denote an area within which something acts, operates, or has power or control: *the **range** of the book's subject; the **ambit** of municipal legislation; information within the **compass** of the article; countries within the political **orbit** of a world power; regulations under the government's **purview**; outside the **reach** of the law; issues within the **scope** of an investigation; outside the **sweep** of federal authority.*

real   **real, actual, true, existent**

These adjectives mean not being imaginary but having verifiable existence. ***Real*** implies authenticity, genuineness, or factuality: *Don't lose the bracelet; it's made of **real** gold. She showed **real** sympathy for my predicament.* ***Actual*** means existing and not merely potential or possible: *"rocks, trees . . . the **actual** world"* (Henry David Thoreau). ***True*** implies consistency with fact, reality, or actuality: *"It is undesirable to believe a proposition when there is no ground whatever for supposing it **true**"* (Bertrand Russell). ***Existent*** applies to what has life or being: *Much of the beluga caviar **existent** in the world is found near the Caspian Sea.*

reap   **reap, garner, gather, glean, harvest**

These verbs mean to collect: ***reaped** what he sowed; **garner** compliments; **gathering** reviews of the book; **glean** information; **harvested** rich rewards.*

reason   **reason, intuition, understanding, judgment**

These nouns refer to the intellectual faculty by which humans seek or attain knowledge or truth. ***Reason*** is the power to think rationally and logically and to draw inferences: *"Mere **reason** is insufficient to convince us of its* [the Christian religion's] *veracity"* (David Hume). ***Intuition*** is perception or comprehension, as of truths or facts, without the use of the rational process: *I trust my **intuitions** when it comes to assessing someone's character.* ***Understanding*** is the faculty by which one understands, often together with the resulting comprehension: *"The greatest dangers to liberty lurk in insidious encroachment by men of zeal, well-meaning but without **understanding**"* (Louis D. Brandeis). ***Judgment*** is the ability to assess situations or circumstances and draw sound conclusions: *"At twenty years of age, the will reigns; at thirty, the wit; and at forty, the **judgment**"* (Benjamin Franklin).

recede   **recede, ebb, retract, retreat**

These verbs mean to move backward or away from a limit or position: *a glacier that has **receded**; waters that **ebb** at low tide; a turtle that **retracted** into its shell; an army that **retreated** to avoid defeat.*
Antonym: advance

refuse   **refuse, decline, reject, spurn, rebuff**

These verbs all mean to be unwilling to accept, consider, or receive someone or something. *Refuse* usually implies determination and often brusqueness: *"The commander . . . refused to discuss questions of right"* (George Bancroft); *"I'll make him an offer he can't refuse"* (Mario Puzo). To *decline* is to refuse politely: *"I declined election to the National Institute of Arts and Letters . . . and now I must decline the Pulitzer Prize"* (Sinclair Lewis). *Reject* suggests the discarding of someone or something as defective or useless; it implies categoric refusal: *"He again offered himself for enlistment and was again rejected"* (Arthur S.M. Hutchinson). To *spurn* is to reject scornfully or contemptuously: *"The more she spurns my love, / The more it grows"* (Shakespeare). *Rebuff* pertains to blunt, often disdainful rejection: *"He had . . . gone too far in his advances, and had been rebuffed"* (Robert Louis Stevenson).

relieve   **relieve, allay, alleviate, assuage, lighten, mitigate, palliate**

These verbs mean to make something less severe or more bearable. To *relieve* is to make more endurable something causing discomfort or distress: *"that misery which he strives in vain to relieve"* (Henry David Thoreau). *Allay* suggests at least temporary relief from what is burdensome or painful: *"This music crept by me upon the waters, / Allaying both their fury and my passion / With its sweet air"* (Shakespeare). *Alleviate* connotes temporary lessening of distress without removal of its cause: *"No arguments shall be wanting on my part that can alleviate so severe a misfortune"* (Jane Austen). To *assuage* is to soothe or make milder: *assuaged his guilt by confessing to the crime.* *Lighten* signifies to make less heavy or oppressive: *legislation that would lighten the taxpayer's burden.* *Mitigate* and *palliate* connote moderating the force or intensity of something that causes suffering: *"I . . . prayed to the Lord to mitigate a calamity"* (John Galt); *"Organizations for writers palliate the writer's loneliness but I doubt if they improve his writing"* (Ernest Hemingway).

remember   **remember, recall, recollect**

These verbs mean to bring an image or a thought back to the mind: *can't remember his name; recalling her kindness; recollected the events leading to the accident.*
Antonym: **forget**

restrain   **restrain, curb, check, bridle, inhibit**

These verbs mean to hold back or keep under control. *Restrain* implies restriction or limitation, as on one's freedom of action: *"a wise and frugal government, which shall restrain men from injuring one another"* (Thomas Jefferson). To *curb* is to restrain as if with reins: *"As a teacher he was rather dull. He curbed his own enthusiasms, finding that they distracted his attention"* (E.M. Forster). *Check* implies arresting or stopping, often suddenly: *"Knowing that Lily disliked to be caressed, she had long ago learned to check her demonstrative impulses toward her friend"* (Edith Wharton). To *bridle* is often to hold in or govern one's emotions or passions: *I tried hard to bridle my anger.* *Inhibit* usually connotes a check on one's actions, thoughts, or emotions: *A fear of strangers* **inhibited** *his ability to travel.*

revere

revere, worship, venerate, adore, idolize

These verbs mean to regard with deep respect, deference, and admiration. *Revere* suggests awe coupled with profound honor: *"At least one third of the population . . .* **reveres** *every sort of holy man"* (Rudyard Kipling). **Worship** connotes an often uncritical devotion: *"[The shortstop]* *was universally* **worshipped** *by fans from the first day he came to Boston"* (Dan Shaughnessy). **Venerate** connotes reverence accorded by virtue especially of dignity or age: *"I* **venerate** *the memory of my grandfather"* (Horace Walpole). To **adore** is to worship with deep, often rapturous love: *The students* **adored** *their caring teacher.* **Idolize** implies regard like that accorded an object of religious devotion: *a general who was* **idolized** *by his troops.*

reverse

reverse, invert, transpose

These verbs mean to change to the opposite position, direction, or course. *Reverse* implies a complete turning about to a contrary position: *We* **reversed** *the arrangement of the sofa and chairs.* To **invert** is basically to turn something upside down or inside out, but the term may imply placing something in a reverse order: **inverted** *the glass;* **invert** *subject and verb to form an interrogative.* **Transpose** applies to altering position in a sequence by reversing or changing the order: *I often misspell* receive *by* **transposing** *the "e" and the "i."*

rich

rich, affluent, moneyed, wealthy

These adjectives mean having an abundant supply of money, property, or possessions of value: *a* **rich** *executive; an* **affluent** *banker;* **moneyed** *heirs;* **wealthy** *corporations.*
Antonym: poor

ridicule

ridicule, mock, taunt, deride

These verbs refer to making another the butt of amusement or mirth. *Ridicule* implies purposeful disparagement: *"My father discouraged me by* **ridiculing** *my performances"* (Benjamin Franklin). To **mock** is to poke fun at someone, often by mimicking and caricaturing speech or actions: *"the bear . . .* [devoured] *the children who* **mocked** *God's servant Elisha for his baldness"* (Garrison Keillor). **Taunt** suggests mocking, insulting, or scornful reproach: *"***taunting*** *him with want of courage to leap into the great pit"* (Daniel Defoe). **Deride** implies scorn and contempt: *"Was all the world in a conspiracy to* **deride** *his failure?"* (Edith Wharton).

rise

rise, ascend, climb, soar, mount

These verbs mean to move upward from a lower to a higher elevation, position, or amount. *Rise* has the widest range of application: *The sun* **rises** *early in the summer. Prices* **rise** *and fall.* **Ascend** frequently suggests a gradual but persistent

rise: *The plane **ascended** steadily until it was out of sight. She **ascended** through the ranks to become CEO.* Similarly, **climb** connotes steady, often effortful progress, as against gravity: *"You **climb** up through the little grades and then get to the top"* (John Updike). **Soar** implies effortless and usually rapid ascent to a great height or noteworthiness: *The fly ball **soared** out of the ballpark. The band's popularity **soared** after the release of the album.* **Mount** connotes a progressive increase to a higher level: *Our expenses **mounted** fearfully.*

sad

sad, melancholy, sorrowful, doleful, woebegone, desolate

These adjectives mean affected with or marked by unhappiness, as that caused by affliction. **Sad** is the most general: *"Better by far you should forget and smile / Than that you should remember and be **sad**"* (Christina Rossetti). **Melancholy** can refer to lingering or habitual somberness or sadness: *a **melancholy** poet's gloomy introspection.* **Sorrowful** applies to emotional pain as that resulting from loss: ***sorrowful** mourners at the funeral.* **Doleful** describes what is mournful or morose: *the **doleful** expression of a reprimanded child.* **Woebegone** suggests grief or wretchedness, especially as reflected in a person's appearance: *"His sorrow . . . made him look . . . haggard and . . . **woebegone**"* (George du Maurier). **Desolate** applies to one that is beyond consolation: *"Now she was **desolate**, a widow in a foreign country"* (Nigel Hamilton).

satisfy

satisfy, answer, fill, fulfill, meet

These verbs mean to be sufficient or to act in adequate measure for something expected or required: ***satisfied** all requirements; **answered** our needs; **fills** a purpose; **fulfilled** their aspirations; **met** her obligations.*

save

save, rescue, reclaim, redeem, deliver

These verbs mean freeing a person or thing from danger, evil, confinement, or servitude. **Save** is the most general: *The smallpox vaccine has **saved** many lives. A police officer **saved** the tourist from being cheated.* **Rescue** usually implies saving from immediate harm or danger by direct action: ***rescue** a rare manuscript from a fire.* **Reclaim** can mean to bring a person back, as from error to virtue or to right or proper conduct: *"To **reclaim** me from this course of life was the sole cause of his journey to London"* (Henry Fielding). To **redeem** is to free someone from captivity or the consequences of sin or error; the term can imply the expenditure of money or effort: *The amount paid to **redeem** the captured duke was enormous.* **Deliver** applies to liberating people from something such as captivity, misery, or peril: *"consigned to a state of wretchedness from which no human efforts will **deliver** them"* (George Washington).

scold

scold, upbraid, berate, revile, vituperate, rail

These verbs mean to reprimand or criticize angrily or vehemently. **Scold** implies reproof: *parents who **scolded** their child for being rude.* **Upbraid** generally suggests a well-founded reproach, as one leveled by an authority: ***upbraided** by the supervisor for habitual tardiness.* **Berate** suggests scolding or rebuking at length:

*"Sergeant Olds . . . **berated** a candidate at the far end of the squad bay for having scuffs on his boots"* (Nathaniel Fick). **Revile** and **vituperate** especially stress the use of scornful or abusive language: *"Hamilton was **reviled** in his time by Jeffersonian democrats as an evil genius in thrall to wealthy aristocracies"* (Walter Isaacson); *"The incensed priests . . . continued to raise their voices, **vituperating** each other in bad Latin"* (Sir Walter Scott). **Rail** suggests bitter, harsh, or denunciatory language: *"Conservatives had **railed** against the liberal interest groups that had attacked* [him]*"* (Jane Mayer).

secret

secret, stealthy, covert, clandestine, furtive, surreptitious, underhand

These adjectives mean deliberately hidden from view or knowledge. **Secret** is the most general: *a desk with a **secret** compartment; **secret** negotiations.* **Stealthy** suggests quiet, cautious deceptiveness intended to escape notice: *heard **stealthy** footsteps on the stairs.* **Covert** describes something that is concealed or disguised: *protested **covert** actions undertaken by the CIA.* **Clandestine** implies stealth and secrecy for the concealment of an often illegal or improper purpose: *a **clandestine** love affair.* **Furtive** suggests the slyness, shiftiness, and evasiveness of a thief: *took a **furtive** glance at the papers on the desk.* Something **surreptitious** is stealthy, furtive, and often unseemly or unethical: *the **surreptitious** recording of a conversation.* **Underhand** implies unfairness, deceit, or slyness as well as secrecy: *achieved success by **underhand** methods.*

see

see, behold, note, notice, remark, espy, descry, observe, contemplate, survey, view, perceive, discern

These verbs refer to being or becoming visually or mentally aware of something. **See,** the most general, can mean merely to use the faculty of sight but more often implies recognition, understanding, or appreciation: *"If I have **seen** further (than . . . Descartes) it is by standing upon the shoulders of Giants"* (Isaac Newton). **Behold** implies gazing at or looking intently upon what is seen: *"My heart leaps up when I **behold** / A rainbow in the sky"* (William Wordsworth). **Note, notice,** and **remark** suggest close, detailed observation, and *note* in particular implies making a careful, systematic mental recording: *Be careful to **note** that we turn left at the church. I **notice** that you're out of sorts. "I **remarked** a fresh colour in her cheeks, and a pinkness over her slender fingers"* (Emily Brontë). **Espy** and **descry** both stress acuteness of sight that permits the detection of something distant or not readily noticeable: *"He drove off about five miles, speeding, before he **espied** a turnoff into a dirt road"* (Flannery O'Connor); *"the lighthouse, which can be **descried** from a distance"* (Michael Strauss). **Observe** emphasizes careful, closely directed attention: *"I saw the pots . . . and **observed** that they did not crack at all"* (Daniel Defoe). **Contemplate** implies looking attentively and thoughtfully: *"It is interesting to **contemplate** an entangled bank, clothed with many plants"* (Charles Darwin). **Survey** stresses comprehensive examination: *"Strickland looked away and idly **surveyed** the ceiling"* (W. Somerset Maugham).

View usually suggests examination with a particular purpose in mind or in a special way: *The medical examiner **viewed** the victim's body.* ***Perceive*** and ***discern*** both imply not only visual recognition but also mental comprehension; ***perceive*** is especially associated with insight, and ***discern,*** with the ability to distinguish, discriminate, and make judgments: *"I plainly **perceive** [that] some objections remain"* (Edmund Burke); *"Your sense of humor would **discern** the hollowness beneath all the pomp and ceremony"* (Edna Ferber).

send **send, dispatch, forward, route, ship, transmit**

These verbs mean to cause to go or be taken to a destination: ***sent** the package by parcel post;* ***dispatched** a union representative to the factory;* ***forwards** the mail to their new address;* ***routed** the soldiers through New York;* ***shipped** his books to his dormitory;* ***transmits** money by cable.*

separate **separate, divide, part, sever, sunder, divorce**

These verbs mean to become or cause to become parted, disconnected, or disunited. ***Separate*** applies both to putting apart and to keeping apart: *"In the darkness and confusion, the bands of these commanders became **separated** from each other"* (Washington Irving). ***Divide*** implies separation by or as if by cutting or splitting into parts or shares; the term often refers to separation into opposing or hostile groups: *We **divided** the orange into segments. "'A house **divided** against itself cannot stand.' I believe this government cannot endure permanently half slave and half free"* (Abraham Lincoln). ***Part*** refers most often to the separation of closely associated persons or things: *"Because . . . nothing that God or Satan could inflict would have **parted** us"* (Emily Brontë). ***Sever*** usually implies abruptness and force: *"His head was nearly **severed** from his body"* (H.G. Wells). ***Sunder*** stresses violent tearing or wrenching apart: *The country was **sundered** by civil war.* ***Divorce*** implies complete separation: *"a priest and a soldier, two classes of men circumstantially **divorced** from the kind and homely ties of life"* (Robert Louis Stevenson).

severe **severe, stern, austere, ascetic, strict**

These adjectives mean unsparing and exacting with respect to discipline or control. ***Severe*** implies adherence to rigorous standards or high principles and often suggests harshness: *"Praise or blame has but a momentary effect on the man whose love of beauty in the abstract makes him a **severe** critic on his own works"* (John Keats). ***Stern*** suggests unyielding disposition, uncompromising resolution, or forbidding appearance or nature: *"She was a **stern** woman who ran the household with precision and an iron hand"* (Margaret Truman). ***Austere*** connotes aloofness or lack of feeling or sympathy, and often rigid morality: *"The captain . . . was an **austere** man that never laughed or smiled that one could see"* (Alan Paton). ***Ascetic*** suggests self-discipline and often renunciation of worldly pleasures for spiritual improvement: *"Be systematically **ascetic** . . . do . . . something for no other reason than that you would rather not do it"* (William James).

Strict means requiring or showing stringent observance of obligations, rules, or standards: *"She was afraid to wake him up because even in his sleep he seemed to be such a **strict** man"* (Eudora Welty).

shake

shake, tremble, quake, quiver, shiver, shudder

These verbs mean to manifest involuntary back-and-forth or up-and-down movement. **Shake** is the most general: *My hand **shook** as I signed the mortgage.* **Tremble** implies quick, rather slight movement, as from excitement, weakness, or anger: *The speaker **trembled** as he denounced his opponents.* **Quake** refers to more violent movement, as that caused by shock or upheaval: *I was so scared that my legs began to **quake**.* **Quiver** suggests a slight, rapid, tremulous movement: *"Her lip **quivered** like that of a child about to cry"* (Booth Tarkington). **Shiver** involves rapid trembling, as of a person experiencing chill: *"as I in hoary winter night stood **shivering** in the snow"* (Robert Southwell). **Shudder** applies chiefly to convulsive shaking caused by fear, horror, or revulsion: *"She starts like one that spies an adder / . . . The fear whereof doth make him shake and **shudder**"* (Shakespeare).

shelter

shelter, cover, retreat, refuge, asylum, sanctuary

These nouns refer to places affording protection, as from danger, or to the state of being protected. **Shelter** usually implies a covered or enclosed area that protects temporarily, as from injury or attack: *built a **shelter** out of pine and hemlock boughs.* **Cover** suggests something that conceals: *traveled under **cover** of darkness.* **Retreat** applies chiefly to a secluded place to which one retires for meditation, peace, or privacy: *a rural cabin that served as a weekend **retreat**.* **Refuge** suggests a place of escape from pursuit or from difficulties that beset one: *"The great advantage of a hotel is that it's a **refuge** from home life"* (George Bernard Shaw). **Asylum** adds to **refuge** the idea of legal protection or of immunity from arrest: *Were the dissidents able to find **asylum** in another country?* **Sanctuary** denotes a sacred or inviolable place of refuge: *political refugees finding **sanctuary** in a monastery.*

shorten

shorten, abbreviate, abridge, curtail, truncate

These verbs mean to reduce something in length, duration, or extent: ***shortened** his life by smoking; **abbreviated** the speech for the television news show; **abridged** the book as an essay; **curtailed** their visit by a week; **truncated** the conversation by saying goodbye.*
Antonym: lengthen

show

show, display, expose, parade, exhibit, flaunt

These verbs mean to present something to view. **Show** is the most general: *"She hated to **show** her feelings"* (John Galsworthy). **Display** often suggests an attempt to present something to best advantage: *The dealer spread the rug out to **display** the pattern.* **Expose** usually involves uncovering something or bringing it out from concealment: *The excavation **exposed** a staggering number of artifacts.* The term can often imply revelation of something better left concealed: *Your comment **exposes** your insensitivity*. **Parade** usually suggests a pretentious or boastful presentation: *"He early discovered that, by **parading** his unhappiness before the multitude, he produced an immense sensation"* (Thomas Macaulay). **Exhibit** implies open presentation that invites inspection: *The museum is **exhibiting** paintings by local artists*. **Flaunt** implies an unabashed, prideful, often arrogant display: *"Every great hostelry **flaunted** the flag of some foreign potentate"* (John Dos Passos).

slide

slide, slip, glide, coast, skid

These verbs mean to move smoothly and continuously, often over a slippery surface. **Slide** usually implies rapid easy movement without loss of contact with the surface: *coal that **slid** down a chute to the cellar*. **Slip** is most often applied to accidental sliding resulting in loss of balance or foothold: ***slipped** on a patch of ice*. **Glide** refers to smooth, free-flowing, seemingly effortless movement: *"four snakes **gliding** up and down a hollow"* (Ralph Waldo Emerson). **Coast** applies especially to downward movement resulting from the effects of gravity or momentum: *The driver let the truck **coast** down the incline*. **Skid** implies an uncontrolled, often sideways sliding caused by a lack of traction: *The bus **skidded** on wet pavement*.

sloppy

sloppy, slovenly, unkempt, slipshod

These adjectives mean marked by an absence of due or proper care or attention. **Sloppy** evokes the idea of careless spilling, spotting, or splashing; it suggests slackness, untidiness, or diffuseness: *a **sloppy** kitchen; **sloppy** dress*. *"I do not see how the **sloppiest** reasoner can evade that"* (H.G. Wells). **Slovenly** implies habitual negligence and a lack of system or thoroughness: *a **slovenly** appearance; **slovenly** inaccuracies*. **Unkempt** stresses dishevelment resulting from a neglectful lack of proper maintenance: *"an unwashed brow, an **unkempt** head of hair"* (Sir Walter Scott). **Slipshod** suggests inattention to detail and a general absence of meticulousness: *"the new owners' camp . . . a **slipshod** and slovenly affair, tent half stretched, dishes unwashed"* (Jack London).

slow

slow, dilatory, leisurely, laggard

These adjectives mean taking more time than is usual or necessary. **Slow** is the least specific: *a **slow** bus; a **slow** heartbeat; **slow** to anger*. **Dilatory** implies lack of promptness caused by delay, procrastination, or indifference: *paid a late fee because I was **dilatory** in paying the bill*. **Leisurely** suggests a relaxed lack of haste: *went for a **leisurely** walk by the river*. **Laggard** implies hanging back or falling behind: *"the horses' **laggard** pace"* (Rudyard Kipling).

small

small, diminutive, little, miniature, miniscule, minute, petite, tiny, wee

These adjectives mean being notably below the average in size or magnitude: *a **small** house; **diminutive** in stature; **little** hands; a **miniature** camera; a*

minuscule amount of rain; *minute* errors; a *petite* figure; *tiny* feet; a *wee* puppy.
Antonym: large

smell

smell, aroma, odor, scent

These nouns denote a quality that can be perceived by the olfactory sense: *the*
*smell of smoke; the **aroma** of frying onions; hospital **odors**; the **scent** of pine*
needles.

sour

sour, acerbic, acid, acidic, tart

These adjectives mean having a taste like that produced by an acid: ***sour** lemons;*
*an **acerbic** vinegar; the **acid** taste of guavas; a lightly **acidic** coffee; **tart** cherries.*

sparing

sparing, frugal, thrifty, economical

These adjectives mean exercising or reflecting care in the use of resources, such
as money. ***Sparing*** stresses restraint, as in expenditure: *a quiet librarian who was*
sparing** of words.* ***Frugal implies self-denial and abstention from luxury: *a **fru-***
gal** diet; a **frugal** monk.* ***Thrifty suggests industry, care, and diligence in conserv-
ing means: *grew up during the Depression and learned to be **thrifty**.* ***Economical***
emphasizes prudence, skillful management, and the avoidance of waste: *an*
***economical** shopper; an **economical** use of energy.*

speak

speak, talk, converse, discourse

These verbs mean to express one's thoughts by uttering words. ***Speak*** and
talk, often interchangeable, are the most general: *"On an occasion of this kind*
*it becomes more than a moral duty to **speak** one's mind. It becomes a pleasure"*
*(Oscar Wilde); "If you want to **talk** about human experience, then let's **talk** about*
it" (Deborah Eisenberg). ***Converse*** stresses interchange of thoughts and ideas:
*"With thee **conversing** I forget all time"* (John Milton). ***Discourse*** usually refers to
formal, extended speech: *"When there was nothing to say, he **discoursed** on the*
nature of silence" (Stacy Schiff).

stem

stem, arise, derive, emanate, flow, issue,
originate, proceed, rise, spring

These verbs mean to come forth or come into being: *customs that **stem** from*
*the past; misery that **arose** from war; rights that **derive** from citizenship; disap-*
*proval that **emanated** from the teacher; happiness that **flows** from their friend-*
*ship; prejudice that **issues** from fear; a proposal that **originated** in the Congress; a*
*mistake that **proceeded** from carelessness; rebellion that **rises** in the provinces; new*
*industries that **spring** from technology.*

stiff

stiff, rigid, inflexible, inelastic, tense

These adjectives describe what is very firm and does not easily bend or give
way. ***Stiff,*** the least specific, refers to what can be flexed only with difficulty (*a*
*brush with **stiff** bristles*); with reference to persons it often suggests a lack of ease,
cold formality, or fixity, as of purpose: *"**stiff** in opinions"* (John Dryden). ***Rigid***

and *inflexible* apply to what cannot be bent without damage or deformation (*a table of **rigid** plastic; an **inflexible** knife blade*); figuratively they describe what does not relent or yield: *"under the dictates of a **rigid** disciplinarian"* (Thomas B. Aldrich); *"In religion the law is written, and **inflexible,** never to do evil"* (Oliver Goldsmith). *Inelastic* refers largely to what will not stretch and spring back without marked physical change: *inelastic construction materials.* By extension it implies an absence of change in the face of changing circumstances: *"My little pension is woefully **inelastic**"* (Flann O'Brien). *Tense* means stretched tight and figuratively applies to what is marked by tautness or strain: *"that **tense** moment of expectation"* (Arnold Bennett).

stop　　**stop, cease, desist, discontinue, halt, quit**

These verbs mean to bring or come to an end: ***stop** arguing; **ceased** crying; **desist** from complaining; **discontinued** the treatment; **halting** the convoy; **quit** laughing.* ***Antonym:*** **start**

strange　　**strange, odd, peculiar, singular, eccentric, outlandish**

These adjectives describe what deviates from the usual or customary. ***Strange*** refers especially to what is unfamiliar, unknown, or inexplicable: *It was **strange** to see so many people out walking around at night.* Something that is ***odd*** fails to accord with what is ordinary, usual, or expected and suggests strangeness: *I find it **odd** that his name is never mentioned in the letter.* Similarly, ***peculiar*** describes what is odd or unusual, but often with an emphasis on distinctness or individuality: *She has a **peculiar** kind of handwriting that is at once pleasant to look at but hard to read.* Even more so, ***singular*** describes what is unique or unparalleled; the term often suggests a quality that arouses curiosity or wonder: *Such poise under pressure is **singular** in one so young.* ***Eccentric*** refers particularly to what is strange and departs strikingly from the conventional: *His musical compositions were innovative but **eccentric.*** ***Outlandish*** suggests alien or bizarre strangeness: *The partygoers wore **outlandish** costumes.*

strength　　**strength, power, might, energy, force**

These nouns denote the capacity to act or work effectively. ***Strength*** refers especially to physical, mental, or moral robustness or vigor: *"enough work to do, and strength **enough** to do the work"* (Rudyard Kipling). ***Power*** is the ability to do something and especially to produce an effect: *"I do not think the United States would come to an end if we lost our **power** to declare an Act of Congress void"* (Oliver Wendell Holmes, Jr.). ***Might*** often implies abundant or extraordinary power: *"He could defend the island against the whole **might** of the German Air Force"* (Winston S. Churchill). ***Energy*** refers especially to a latent source of power: *"The same **energy** of character which renders a man a daring villain would have rendered him useful to society, had that society been well organized"* (Mary Wollstonecraft). ***Force*** is the application of power or strength: *"the overthrow of our institutions by **force** and violence"* (Charles Evans Hughes).

subject   **subject, matter, topic, theme**

These nouns denote the principal idea or point of a speech, a piece of writing, or an artistic work. *Subject* is the most general: "*Well, honor is the **subject** of my story*" (Shakespeare). *Matter* refers to the material that is the object of thought or discourse: "*This distinction seems to me to go to the root of the **matter**"* (William James). A *topic* is a subject of discussion, argument, or conversation: "*They would talk of . . . fashionable **topics**, such as pictures, taste, Shakespeare*" (Oliver Goldsmith). *Theme* refers especially to an idea, a point of view, or a perception that is developed and expanded on in a work of art: "*To produce a mighty book, you must choose a mighty **theme**"* (Herman Melville).

sufficient   **sufficient, acceptable, adequate, enough, satisfactory**

These adjectives mean being what is needed without being in excess: *has **sufficient** income to retire comfortably; made **acceptable** grades; put in an **adequate** supply of wood; drew **enough** water to fill the tub; offered a **satisfactory** sum for the property.*
Antonym: **insufficient**

suggest   **suggest, imply, hint, intimate, insinuate**

These verbs mean to convey thoughts or ideas by indirection. *Suggest* refers to the calling of something to mind as the result of an association of ideas: "*Are you **suggesting** that I invited or enticed Kevin here knowing that my husband planned to be away?*" (Mary Higgins Clark). To *imply* is to suggest a thought or an idea by letting it be inferred from something else, such as a statement, that is more explicit: *The effusive praise the professor heaped on one of the students began to **imply** disapproval of the rest.* *Hint* refers to an oblique or covert suggestion that often contains clues: *The news article **hinted** that his resignation was not voluntary.* *Intimate* applies to indirect, subtle expression that often reflects discretion, tact, or reserve: *She **intimated** that her neighbors were having marital problems.* To *insinuate* is to suggest something, usually something unpleasant, in a covert, sly, and underhanded manner: *The columnist **insinuated** that the candidate raised money unethically.*

summit   **summit, peak, pinnacle, acme, apex, zenith, climax**

These nouns all mean the highest point. *Summit* denotes the highest level attainable: "*His six years with the canal company marked the **summit** of his career as a company man*" (Simon Winchester). *Peak* usually refers to the uppermost or most intense point: "*It was the **peak** of summer in the Berkshires*" (Saul Bellow). *Pinnacle* denotes a towering height, as of achievement: *The articulation of the theory of relativity catapulted Einstein to the **pinnacle** of his profession.* *Acme* refers to an ultimate point, as of perfection: *The artist's talents were at their **acme** when this work was created.* *Apex* is the culminating point: *The movie begins with the dictator at the **apex** of his power.* *Zenith* is the point of highest achievement, most complete development, or greatest power: "*Chivalry was then in its* *zenith*" (Henry Hallam). *Climax* refers to the point of greatest strength, effect, or intensity that marks the endpoint of an ascending process: *The government's collapse was the **climax** of a series of constitutional crises.*

surprise **surprise, astonish, amaze, astound, dumbfound, flabbergast**

These verbs mean to affect a person strongly as being unexpected or unusual. To **surprise** is to fill with often sudden wonder or disbelief as being unanticipated or out of the ordinary: "*Never tell people* how *to do things. Tell them* what *to do and they will **surprise** you with their ingenuity*" (George S. Patton). **Astonish** suggests overwhelming surprise: *The sight of such an enormous crowd **astonished** us.* **Amaze** implies astonishment and often bewilderment: *The violinist's virtuosity has **amazed** audiences all over the world.* **Astound** connotes shock, as from something unprecedented in one's experience: *We were **astounded** at the beauty of the mountains.* **Dumbfound** adds to **astound** the suggestion of perplexity and often speechlessness: *His question **dumbfounded** me, and I could not respond.* **Flabbergast** is used as a more colorful equivalent of **astound, astonish,** or **amaze**: "*He was utterly **flabbergasted** by the accusation and for a few moments he was quite unable to reply*" (Alexander McCall Smith).

swerve **swerve, depart, deviate, digress, diverge, stray, veer**

These verbs mean to turn away from a straight path or established pattern, as of thought or action: *a gaze that never **swerved**; won't **depart** from family traditions; **deviated** from the original plan; **digressed** from the main topic; opinions that **diverged**; **strays** from the truth; a conversation that **veered** away from sensitive issues.*

swing **swing, oscillate, sway, rock, vibrate, waver**

These verbs mean literally to move one way and then another, usually back and forth or to and fro. Some verbs often see figurative use: **Swing** usually applies to arclike movement of something attached at one extremity and free at the other: *The ship's lanterns **swung** violently in the raging storm.* Figuratively, it denotes difficulty to decide or act from being drawn by conflicting purposes or emotions: "*She **swung** between disbelief and dread*" (Denise Grady). **Oscillate** similarly refers to a steady back-and-forth motion, as that of a pendulum, and also can indicate figurative vacillation: "*a king . . . **oscillating** between fear of Rome and desire of independence*" (Walter Besant). **Sway** suggests the movement of something unsteady, light, or flexible: "*thousands of the little yellow blossoms all **swaying** to the light wind*" (W.H. Hudson). To **rock** is to swing gently or rhythmically or sway or tilt violently: "*The ruins of the ancient church seemed actually to **rock** and threaten to fall*" (Sir Walter Scott). **Vibrate** implies quick periodic oscillations; it can also suggest trembling, pulsating, or quivering: "*Music, when soft voices die, / **Vibrates** in the memory*" (Percy Bysshe Shelley). **Waver** suggests unsteady, uncertain movement: "*Through the hard, driving rain the sentinel birches **wavered** like pale, elongated ghosts*" (Melissa Hardy). It also suggests inconstancy or irresolution of feeling or action: *"I have a friend who was reared to believe, and he does. But his faith has **wavered**"* (Dana Tierney).

tardy **tardy, late, overdue**

These adjectives mean not arriving, occurring, acting, or done at the scheduled, expected, or usual time: ***tardy*** *in making a dental appointment;* ***late*** *for the plane; an* ***overdue*** *bus.*
Antonym: prompt

task **task, job, chore, assignment**

These nouns denote a piece of work that one must do. A ***task*** is a well-defined responsibility that is usually imposed by another and that may be burdensome: *I stayed at work late to finish the* ***task*** *at hand.* ***Job*** often suggests a specific short-term undertaking: *"did little* ***jobs*** *about the house with skill"* (W.H. Auden). ***Chore*** generally denotes a minor or routine job: *The farmer's morning* ***chores*** *included milking the cows.* ***Assignment*** generally denotes a task allotted by a person in authority: *His homework* ***assignment*** *involved writing an essay.*

teach **teach, instruct, educate, train, school, discipline, drill**

These verbs mean to impart knowledge or skill. ***Teach*** is the most widely applicable: ***taught*** *the child to draw;* ***taught*** *literature at the college.* ***Instruct*** often suggests training in some special field or skill: ***instructed*** *the undergraduates in music theory.* ***Educate*** often implies formal instruction but especially stresses the development of innate capacities: *"We are* ***educated*** *by others . . . and this cultivation, mingling with our innate disposition, is the soil in which our desires, passions, and motives grow"* (Mary Shelley). ***Train*** suggests concentration on particular skills intended to fit a person for a desired role: ***trained*** *the vocational students to be computer technicians.* ***School*** often implies an arduous training process: *"He took young Deanie under his wing and* ***schooled*** *him in the art of ambidextrous gunplay"* (T.J. English). ***Discipline*** usually refers to the teaching of control, especially self-control: ***disciplined*** *myself to exercise every day.* ***Drill*** implies rigorous instruction or training, usually by repetition: ***drilled*** *the students by having them recite the multiplication tables.*

temporary **temporary, acting, interim, provisional**

These adjectives mean assuming the duties of another for the time being: *a* ***temporary*** *chairperson; the* ***acting*** *dean; an* ***interim*** *administration; a* ***provisional*** *mayor.*
Antonym: permanent

tendency **tendency, trend, current, drift, tenor**

These nouns refer to the direction or course of an action or thought. ***Tendency*** implies a predisposition to proceed in a particular way: *"The* ***tendency*** *of our own day is . . . towards firm, solid, verifiable knowledge"* (William H. Mallock). ***Trend*** often applies to a general or prevailing direction, especially within a particular sphere: *"the **trend** of religious thought in recent times"* (James Harvey Robinson). ***Current*** suggests a course or flow, as of opinion, especially one representative of a given time or place: *"the whole **current** of modern feeling"* (James Bryce). A ***drift*** is a tendency that seems driven by a current of events: *a **drift** toward anarchy as the government collapsed.* ***Tenor*** implies a general or ongoing course: *"The tempo, the **tenor** of life on the mountain and around the mine began to change"* (Anita Desai).

think

think, cerebrate, cogitate, reason, reflect

These verbs mean to use the powers of the mind, as in conceiving ideas or drawing inferences: ***thought** before answering; sat in front of the fire **cerebrating**; cogitates about business problems; **reasons** clearly; took time to **reflect** before deciding.*

thoughtful

thoughtful, considerate, attentive, solicitous

These adjectives mean having or showing concern for the well-being of others. Although ***thoughtful*** and ***considerate*** are often used interchangeably, ***thoughtful*** implies a tendency to anticipate needs or wishes, whereas ***considerate*** stresses sensitivity to another's feelings: *a **thoughtful** friend who brought me soup when I was sick; **considerate**, quiet neighbors.* ***Attentive*** suggests devoted, assiduous attention: *an excellent host who was **attentive** to the needs of his guests.* ***Solicitous*** implies deep concern, sometimes accompanied by worry: *a mother who is very **solicitous** of her asthmatic child.*

throw

throw, cast, hurl, fling, pitch, toss

These verbs mean to propel something through the air with a motion of the hand or arm. ***Throw*** is the least specific: ***throwing** a ball; **threw** the life preserver to the struggling swimmer.* ***Cast*** usually refers to throwing something light, often in discarding it: *"She **cast** the unpleasant, pricking garments from her"* (Kate Chopin). ***Hurl*** and ***fling*** mean to throw with great force: *"Him the Almighty Power / **Hurl'd** headlong flaming from th' Ethereal Sky"* (John Milton); *"He **flung** the magazine across the room, knocking a picture frame from the bookcase and surprising himself with this sudden burst of anger"* (Yiyun Li). ***Pitch*** often means to throw with careful aim: *"He **pitched** the canteen to the man behind him"* (Cormac McCarthy). ***Toss*** usually means to throw lightly or casually: *"Campton **tossed** the card away"* (Edith Wharton).

tire

tire, weary, fatigue, exhaust

These verbs mean to cause or undergo depletion of energy, strength, or interest. ***Tire*** often suggests a state resulting from exertion, excess, dullness, or ennui: *"When a man is tired of London, he is **tired** of life"* (Samuel Johnson). ***Weary*** often implies dissatisfaction, as that resulting from what is irksome or boring: *found the long journey **wearying**; soon **wearied** of their constant bickering.* ***Fatigue*** implies great weariness, as that caused by stress or overwork: *"**fatigued** by an endless rotation of thought and wild alarms"* (Mary Wollstonecraft). To ***exhaust*** means to wear out completely, and it connotes total draining of physical

or emotional strength: *"Like all people who try to **exhaust** a subject, he exhausted his listeners"* (Oscar Wilde); *"Following a similar 'tempest' he had . . . actually apologized to me for his misbehavior . . . Scenes such as I had just been a participant in fractured my spirit, **exhausted** me"* (William Styron).

tireless   tireless, indefatigable, unflagging, untiring, unwearied, weariless

These adjectives mean having or showing a capacity for persistent or prolonged effort: *a **tireless** worker; an **indefatigable** advocate of human rights; **unflagging** pursuit of excellence; **untiring** energy; an **unwearied** researcher; a **weariless** defender of freedom of the press.*

trust   trust, faith, confidence, reliance

These nouns denote a feeling of certainty that a person or thing will not fail. ***Trust*** implies depth and assurance of feeling that is often based on inconclusive evidence: *The mayor vowed to justify the **trust** the electorate had placed in him.* ***Faith*** connotes unquestioning, often emotionally charged belief: *"Often enough our **faith** beforehand in an uncertified result is the only thing that makes the result come true"* (William James). ***Confidence*** frequently implies stronger grounds for assurance: *"The experience . . . made me want to be a surgeon—not an amateur handed the knife for a brief moment but someone with the **confidence** and ability to proceed as if it were routine"* (Atul Gawande). ***Reliance*** connotes a confident and trustful commitment to another: *"What **reliance** could they place on the protection of a prince so recently their enemy?"* (William Hickling Prescott).

turn   turn, circle, rotate, revolve, gyrate, spin, whirl, eddy, swirl

These verbs mean to move a circle. ***Turn*** and ***circle*** are the most general: *The mechanic made sure the wheels **turned** properly. Seagulls **circled** above the ocean.* ***Rotate*** refers to movement around an object's own axis or center: *Earth **rotates** on its axis once each day.* ***Revolve*** involves orbital movement: *Earth **revolves** around the sun.* ***Gyrate*** suggests revolving in or as if in a spiral course: *The top **gyrated** on the counter and slowly came to a stop.* To ***spin*** is to rotate rapidly, often within a narrow compass: *"He . . . **spun** round, flung up his arms, and fell on his back, shot through"* (John Galsworthy). ***Whirl*** applies to rapid or forceful revolution or rotation: *During the blizzard, snowflakes **whirled** down from the sky.* ***Eddy*** denotes rapid circular movement like that of a whirlpool: *Storm clouds **eddied** overhead.* ***Swirl*** can connote a graceful undulation, spiral, or whorl: *The leaves **swirled** in the wind.*

uncertainty   uncertainty, doubt, dubiety, skepticism

These nouns refer to the condition of being unsure about someone or something. ***Uncertainty***, the least forceful, merely denotes a lack of assurance or conviction: *I regarded my decision with growing **uncertainty**.* ***Doubt*** and ***dubiety*** imply a questioning state of mind: *"**Doubt** is part of all religion"* (Isaac Bashevis

Singer); "*He is . . . earnest, his earnestness seasoned with the proper amount of* **dubiety** *and humor*" (Joseph Epstein). **Skepticism** generally suggests an instinctive or habitual tendency to question and demand proof: "*A wise* **skepticism** *is the first attribute of a good critic*" (James Russell Lowell).

understand   **understand, comprehend, apprehend, grasp**

These verbs denote perception of the nature and significance of something. **Understand** is the most general and can apply to a range of situations or degrees of perception: **understood** *the directions;* **understands** *only a little spoken Spanish; couldn't* **understand** *what I did wrong.* It can also refer to the thorough knowledge gained by close experience: "*No one who has not had the responsibility can really* **understand** *what it is like to be President*" (Harry S. Truman). **Comprehend** stresses wide or thorough perception: "*To* **comprehend** *is to know a thing as well as that thing can be known*" (John Donne). **Apprehend** denotes both mental and intuitive awareness: "*Intelligence is quickness to* **apprehend**" (Alfred North Whitehead). To **grasp** is to seize an idea firmly: "*We have* **grasped** *the mystery of the atom and rejected the Sermon on the Mount*" (Omar N. Bradley).

urgent   **urgent, exigent, pressing, imperative**

These adjectives mean compelling immediate attention. **Urgent** often implies that a matter takes precedence over others: "*For I ride on an errand most* **urgent**, *and with the first light of morning we must go*" (J.R.R. Tolkien). **Exigent** and **pressing** suggest an urgency that requires prompt action: "*When once disease was introduced into the rural districts, its effects appeared more horrible, more* **exigent**, *and more difficult to cure, than in towns*" (Mary Shelley); "*The danger now became too* **pressing** *to admit of longer delay*" (James Fenimore Cooper). **Imperative** implies a need or demand whose fulfillment cannot be deferred: "*The stricken countries of Europe needed everything and could afford to buy nothing. Financial help was* **imperative**" (David McCullough).

vain   **vain, empty, hollow, idle, otiose**

These adjectives mean lacking value or substance: **vain** *regrets;* **empty** *pleasures;* **hollow** *threats;* **idle** *dreams;* **otiose** *theoretical discussions.*

vociferous   **vociferous, blatant, boisterous, strident, clamorous**

These adjectives mean conspicuously and usually offensively loud. **Vociferous** suggests a noisy outcry, as of vehement protest: **vociferous** *complaints.* **Blatant** connotes coarse or vulgar noisiness: "*students demanding unlimited freedom in a noisy and* **blatant** *protest against all university authority*" (Thomas Anthony Harris). **Boisterous** implies unrestrained noise, tumult, and often rowdiness: **boisterous** *youths.* **Strident** stresses offensive harshness, shrillness, or discordance: *a legislator with a* **strident** *voice.* Something **clamorous** is both vociferous and sustained: *a* **clamorous** *uproar.*

wander | **wander, ramble, roam, rove, range, meander, stray, gallivant, gad**

These verbs mean to move about at random or without destination or purpose. *Wander* and *ramble* stress the absence of a fixed course or goal: *The professor wandered down the hall lost in thought.* *"They would go off together, rambling along the river"* (John Galsworthy). *Roam* and *rove* emphasize freedom of movement, often over a wide area: *"Herds of horses and cattle roamed at will over the plain"* (George W. Cable); *"For ten long years I roved about, living first in one capital, then another"* (Charlotte Brontë). *Range* suggests wandering in all directions: *"a large hunting party known to be ranging the prairie"* (Francis Parkman). *Meander* suggests leisurely wandering over an irregular or winding course: *"He meandered to and fro . . . observing the manners and customs of Hillport society"* (Arnold Bennett). *Stray* refers to deviation from a proper course or area: *"The camels strayed to graze on the branches of distant acacias"* (Jeffrey Tayler). *Gallivant* refers to wandering in search of pleasure: *gallivanted all over the city during our visit.* *Gad* suggests restlessness: *gadded about unaccompanied in foreign places.*

waste | **waste, blow, dissipate, fritter, squander**

These verbs mean to spend or expend without restraint and often to no avail: *wasted my inheritance; blew a fortune at the casino; dissipated their energies in pointless argument; frittering away her entire allowance; squandered his talent on writing jingles.*
Antonym: **save**

whole | **whole, all, entire, gross, total**

These adjectives mean including every constituent or individual: *a whole town devastated by an earthquake; all the class going on a field trip; entire shipments lost by the distributor; gross income; the total cost of the project.*
Antonym: **partial**

work | **work, labor, toil, drudgery, travail**

These nouns refer to physical or mental effort expended to produce or accomplish something. *Work* is the most widely applicable: *hard work in the fields; did some work around the house on weekends; a first draft that still needs work.* *Labor* usually implies human work, especially of a hard physical or intellectual nature: *a construction job that involves heavy labor.* *"All scholarly work builds on the cumulative labors of others"* (Jerome Karabel). *Toil* applies principally to strenuous, fatiguing labor: *"a spirited woman of intellect condemned to farmhouse toil"* (Cynthia Ozick). *Drudgery* suggests dull, wearisome, or monotonous work: *"the drudgery of penning definitions and marking quotations for transcription"* (Thomas Macaulay). *Travail* connotes arduous work involving pain or suffering: *"prisoners of the splendor and travail of the earth"* (Henry Beston).

yell

yell, bawl, bellow, holler, howl, roar, shout, whoop

These verbs mean to say with or make a loud cry: *troops **yelling** as they attacked; a drum major **bawling** out orders; a coach **bellowing** with rage; a sailor **hollering** a warning; a patient **howling** with pain; a crowd **roaring** its disapproval; fans **shouting** their enthusiasm; children **whooping** at play.*

yield

yield, relent, bow, defer, submit, capitulate, succumb

These verbs all mean to give in to what one can no longer oppose or resist. **Yield** has the widest application: *My neighbor won't **yield** to reason. "The child . . . soon **yielded** to the drowsiness"* (Charles Dickens). To **relent** is to moderate the harshness or severity of an attitude or decision: *"The captain at last **relented,** and told him that he might make himself at home"* (Herman Melville). **Bow** suggests giving way in defeat or through courtesy: *"**Bow** and accept the end/Of a love"* (Robert Frost). To **defer** is to yield out of respect for or in recognition of another's authority, knowledge, or judgment: *"Philip . . . had the good sense to **defer** to the long experience and the wisdom of his father"* (William Hickling Prescott). **Submit** implies giving way out of necessity, as after futile or unsuccessful resistance: *"obliged to **submit** to those laws which are imposed upon us"* (Abigail Adams). **Capitulate** implies surrender to pressure, force, compulsion, or inevitability: *"I am ashamed to think how easily we **capitulate** to badges and names, to large societies and dead institutions"* (Ralph Waldo Emerson). **Succumb** strongly suggests submission to something overpowering or overwhelming: *"If a soldier stayed on the line long enough, he would **succumb** to mental stresses if he was not physically injured first"* (Roger J. Spiller).

young

young, youthful, adolescent, immature, juvenile, childish, puerile, infantile

These adjectives relate to an early stage of growth or development and to its accompanying characteristics. **Young** is the most general, applying to various periods of life, generally before middle age, as well as to inanimate entities: *a **young** child; a **young** couple; a **young** galaxy.* It can suggest a youthful attitude or outlook regardless of chronological age: ***young** at heart.* **Youthful** suggests the positive characteristics, such as enthusiasm, freshness, or energy, that are traditionally associated with youth: *approached the task with **youthful** ardor.* **Adolescent** connotes the physical and especially mental or emotional characteristics of those between childhood and maturity; it is generally not disparaging except when used of an adult: ***adolescent** insecurity; an **adolescent** outburst from the trial lawyer.* **Immature** is more clearly judgmental, implying that someone falls short of an expected level of mental or emotional development for his or her age: *an emotionally **immature** adult.* **Juvenile** suggests the immaturity usually associated with adolescents, but it can convey at attitude of tolerance as well as criticism: *the **juvenile** pranks of the conventioneers.* **Childish** is similar to **juvenile** but with a younger frame of reference, often suggesting selfishness, stubbornness, or lack of restraint: *a committee member with a **childish** need to have the last word.* However, it can also suggest such positive qualities of children as innocence and wholeheartedness: *took **childish** delight in tending his garden.* ***Puerile*** and ***infantile*** are used derogatorily to suggest extreme immaturity, especially with regard to social manners: *a **puerile** joke; an **infantile** boast.*

zest

zest, gusto, relish

These nouns denote keen, hearty pleasure or appreciation: *ate the delicious meal with **zest**; told the amusing story with **gusto**; has no **relish** for repetitive work.*

Index

This alphabetical index shows you where you can find synonyms and antonyms in your thesaurus. For example, the index entry

simple *see* easy

indicates that to find synonyms for the word *simple*, you must look under the entry for *easy*. There you will find other synonyms, in this case *effortless* and *facile*.

Headwords of entries are listed in color by themselves in the same index. For example, the index entry

recede

shows that *recede* is an entry in the thesaurus at which you will find synonyms for *recede*.

If a headword of an entry also appears at another entry as a synonym, the index entry will be repeated. For example, the index entries

bright

bright *see* intelligent

indicate that *bright* is an entry in the thesaurus and the word *bright* also appears at the entry for *intelligent*.

Some words appear as synonyms in more than one entry. For example, the index entry

conform *see* adapt, correspond

indicates that the word conform appears at the entries for both *adapt* and *correspond*.

Antonyms are marked by the phrase *see antonym at*. For example, the index entry

deliberation *see antonym at* haste

indicates that to find *deliberation* listed as an antonym, you must look under the entry for *haste*, where you will find *deliberation*.

abash *see* embarrass
abate *see* decrease
abbreviate *see* shorten
abridge *see* shorten
absurd *see* foolish
abundant *see* plentiful
accede *see* assent
acceptable *see* average
acclaim *see* praise
accommodate *see* adapt, contain
accompany
accomplish *see* perform
accomplished *see* proficient
accord *see* correspond
accumulate *see* gather
acerbic *see* sour
achieve *see* perform
acid *see* sour
acidic *see* sour
acknowledge
acme *see* summit
acquiesce *see* assent
acting *see* temporary
active
actual *see* real
adapt
adept *see* proficient
adequate *see* sufficient
adjust *see* adapt
admit *see* acknowledge
admonish
adolescent *see* young
adore *see* revere
adroit *see* dexterous
advance *see antonym at* recede
adventuresome *see* adventurous
adventurous
affect *see* move
affectation
affecting *see* moving
affliction *see* burden
affluent *see* rich
affront *see* offend
aggravate *see* annoy
agitate
agree *see* assent, correspond
agreement
aim
aim *see* intention
air *see* affectation

alarm *see* fear, frighten
albatross *see* burden
alert *see* careful
all *see* whole
allay *see* relieve
alleviate *see* relieve
ally *see* partner
alone
alternative *see* choice
amalgamate *see* mix
amass *see* gather
amaze *see* surprise
ambiguous
ambit *see* range
amend *see* correct
ample *see* plentiful
amuse
ancient *see* old
anger
angry
animosity *see* enmity
animus *see* enmity
annihilate
annoy
answer
answer *see* satisfy
antagonism *see* enmity
antediluvian *see* old
anticipate *see* expect
antipathy *see* enmity
antiquated *see* old
antique *see* old
ape *see* imitate
apex *see* summit
apparent
appease *see* pacify
apportion *see* distribute
appreciate
apprehend *see* understand
apprehension *see* fear
arcane *see* mysterious
archaic *see* old
arctic *see* cold
ardor *see* passion
argue
arise *see* stem
aroma *see* smell
arouse *see* provoke
artless *see* naive
ascend *see* rise
ascetic *see* severe
ascribe *see* attribute

ask
assail *see* attack
assault *see* attack
assemble *see* gather
assent
assiduous *see* diligent
assign *see* attribute
assignment *see* task
assuage *see* relieve
astonish *see* surprise
astound *see* surprise
asylum *see* shelter
attack
attentive *see* careful, thoughtful
attest *see* indicate
attribute
attribute *see* quality
audacious *see* adventurous, brave
augment *see* increase
augur *see* foretell
august *see* grand
austere *see* severe
authentic
authenticate *see* confirm
average
avert *see* prevent
avoid *see* evade
await *see* expect
awake *see* aware
aware

badger *see* harass
bailiwick *see* field
balloon *see* bulge
bamboozle *see* deceive
ban *see* forbid
bargain *see* agreement
barren *see* futile
base
baseless
basis *see* base
batter *see* attack
bawl *see* cry, yell
bear *see* produce
bearing *see* behavior
beat *see* defeat
beautiful
befall *see* happen
befoul *see* contaminate
begin

beginning
beguile *see* charm
behavior
behold *see* see
belittle *see* disparage
bellicose *see* belligerent
belligerent
bellow *see* yell
belly *see* bulge
benevolent
berate *see* scold
beset *see* attack
bespeak *see* indicate
betide *see* happen
betoken *see* indicate
bewilder *see* perplex
bewitch *see* charm
bicker *see* argue
big *see* large
birth *see* beginning
blank *see* empty
blatant *see* vociferous
blemish
blend *see* mix
block
blow *see* waste
blubber *see* cry
blue *see* depressed
blunt *see* gruff
boast
boil
boisterous *see* vociferous
bold *see* brave
bona fide *see* authentic
bootless *see* futile
border
boring
bother *see* annoy
bow *see* yield
brag *see* boast
brave
brawl
brawny *see* muscular
breach
break
break *see* opportunity
breakable *see* fragile
bridle *see* restrain
bright
bright *see* intelligent
brilliant *see* bright, intelligent
brink *see* border

brittle *see* fragile
brood
brusque *see* gruff
bulge
bullheaded *see* obstinate
burden
burly *see* muscular
burn
burst *see* break
business
busy *see* active

cache *see* hide
calculate
calm
cancel *see* erase
candid *see* frank
capitulate *see* yield
captivate *see* charm
care
careful
careless
carp *see* quibble
case *see* example
cast *see* throw
casual *see* chance
catch
cavil *see* quibble
cease *see* stop
ceaseless *see* continual
celebrate *see* observe
celebrated *see* famous
celebrity
celerity *see* haste
censure *see* criticize
cerebrate *see* think
chagrin *see* embarrass
chance
chance *see* happen, opportunity
chaperone *see* accompany
char *see* burn
character *see* disposition, quality
charge *see* care
charitable *see* benevolent
charity *see* mercy
charm
check *see* restrain
cheerful *see* glad
cherish *see* appreciate
chief

childish *see* young
chilly *see* cold
choice
chore *see* task
chubby *see* fat
churn *see* agitate
circle *see* turn
clamor *see* noise
clamorous *see* vociferous
clandestine *see* secret
clash *see* conflict
clear *see* apparent
clear-cut *see* apparent
clemency *see* mercy
climax *see* summit
climb *see* rise
cloak *see* hide
close *see* complete
coalesce *see* mix
coast *see* slide
coerce *see* force
cogitate *see* think
cognizant *see* aware
coincide *see* correspond
coincident *see* contemporary
cold
colleague *see* partner
collect *see* gather
colorless *see* dull
colossal *see* enormous
combat *see* oppose
combative *see* belligerent
combine *see* join
comely *see* beautiful
comfortable
commemorate *see* observe
commence *see* begin
commend *see* praise
commerce *see* business
commiseration *see* pity
common
compact *see* agreement
compass *see* range
compassion *see* pity
compel *see* force
complete
complex
complicated *see* complex
component *see* element
comportment *see* behavior
comprehend *see* include, understand

comprise *see* include
compute *see* calculate
conceal *see* hide
concede *see* acknowledge
concept *see* idea
conception *see* idea
conciliate *see* pacify
conclude *see* complete, decide
concomitant *see* contemporary
concur *see* assent
concurrent *see* contemporary
condemn *see* criticize
condolence *see* pity
condone *see* forgive
conduct *see* accompany, behavior
confederate *see* partner
confess *see* acknowledge
confidence *see* trust
confirm
conflict
conform *see* adapt, correspond
confound *see* perplex
congregate *see* gather
connect *see* join
conquer *see* defeat
conscientious *see* diligent
conscious *see* aware
consent *see* assent
consequence *see* effect, importance
considerate *see* thoughtful
conspicuous *see* noticeable
constant *see* continual, faithful
constituent *see* element
construe *see* explain
consume *see* eat
consummate *see* perfect
contain
contaminate
contemplate *see* see
contemporaneous *see* contemporary
contemporary
contention *see* conflict
contest *see* oppose
continual
continuous *see* continual

contort *see* distort
contour *see* form, outline
converse *see* speak
convulse *see* agitate
cool *see* cold
copious *see* plentiful
copy *see* imitate
corpulent *see* fat
correct
correspond
corroborate *see* confirm
courageous *see* brave
covenant *see* agreement
cover *see* shelter
covert *see* secret
covet *see* desire
cozy *see* comfortable
crack *see* break, joke
crave *see* desire
credit *see* attribute
critical *see* indispensable
criticize
cross *see* burden
crow *see* boast
crush
cry
cryptic *see* mysterious
curb *see* restrain
current *see* flow, tendency
curt *see* gruff
curtail *see* shorten
custody *see* care
custom *see* habit

daredevil *see* adventurous
daring *see* adventurous
dark
dauntless *see* brave
dawn *see* beginning
deadly *see* fatal
deal *see* agreement, distribute
deceitful *see* dishonest
deceive
decide
decline *see* refuse
decrease
decry *see* criticize
defeat
defect *see* blemish
defend
defer *see* yield

deform *see* distort
deft *see* dexterous
dejected *see* depressed
delectable *see* delicious
delete *see* erase
deliberation *see antonym at* haste
delicate *see* exquisite
delicious
deliver *see* save
delude *see* deceive
demeanor *see* behavior
demolish *see* destroy
denigrate *see* disparage
denounce *see* criticize
depart *see* swerve
deportment *see* behavior
depreciate *see* disparage
depressed
derelict *see* negligent
deride *see* ridicule
derive *see* stem
describe
descry *see* see
deserve *see* earn
design *see* figure
desire
desist *see* stop
desolate *see* sad
despondent *see* depressed
destroy
desultory *see* chance
determine *see* decide
detestable *see* hateful
deviate *see* swerve
device *see* figure
devour *see* eat
dexterous
difference
digress *see* swerve
dilatory *see* slow
diligent
dim *see* dark
diminish *see* decrease
diminutive *see* small
din *see* noise
direct *see* aim
dirty
disappear
discern *see* see
discipline *see* teach
discomfit *see* embarrass

disconcert *see* embarrass
disconsolate *see* depressed
discontinue *see* stop
discord *see* conflict
discourse *see* speak
discrepancy *see* difference
disengage *see* extricate
disentangle *see* extricate
disgusting *see* offensive
dishonest
disparage
dispatch *see* haste, send
dispense *see* distribute
dispirited *see* depressed
display *see* show
disposition
dissension *see* conflict
dissimilarity *see* difference
dissipate *see* waste
distinct *see* apparent
distinction *see* difference
distort
distribute
diverge *see* swerve
divergence *see* difference
divert *see* amuse
divide *see* distribute,
   separate
divine *see* foretell
divorce *see* separate
dole *see* distribute
doleful *see* sad
domain *see* field
donnybrook *see* brawl
dormant *see* inactive
doubt *see* uncertainty
downcast *see* depressed
downhearted *see* depressed
drab *see* dull
dread *see* fear
drift *see* tendency
drill *see* teach
drudgery *see* work
dry *see* sour
dubiety *see* uncertainty
dull
dumbfound *see* surprise
dupe *see* deceive
dusky *see* dark
dwell *see* brood
dwindle *see* decrease
dynamic *see* active

earn
easy
easy *see* comfortable
eat
ebb *see* recede
eccentric *see* strange
economical *see* sparing
eddy *see* turn
edge *see* border
educate *see* teach
effect
effortless *see* easy
effulgent *see* bright
elastic *see* flexible
eleemosynary *see* benevolent
elegant *see* exquisite
element
elucidate *see* explain
elude *see* evade
emanate *see* stem
embarrass
embrace *see* include
eminent *see* famous
empathy *see* pity
empty
empty *see* vain
enchant *see* charm
encompass *see* include
end *see* *antonym at* beginning
end *see* complete, intention
endanger
energetic *see* active
energy *see* strength
enigmatic *see* mysterious
enlarge *see* increase
enmesh *see* catch
enmity
enormous
enough *see* sufficient
ensnare *see* catch
ensue *see* follow
entangle *see* catch
entertain *see* amuse
entire *see* whole
entrance *see* charm
entrap *see* catch
episode *see* occurrence
equipment
equitable *see* fair
equivocal *see* ambiguous
erase

erudition *see* knowledge
eschew *see* evade
escort *see* accompany
esoteric *see* mysterious
espy *see* see
essential *see* indispensable
esteem *see* appreciate
eternal *see* continual
ethical *see* moral
evade
evanesce *see* disappear
evaporate *see* disappear
even *see* level
event *see* occurrence
evident *see* apparent
example
examine *see* ask
exceed *see* excel
excel
excessive
excite *see* provoke
excuse *see* forgive
execute *see* perform
exemplar *see* ideal
exhaust *see* tire
exhibit *see* show
exigent *see* urgent
existent *see* real
expand *see* increase
expect
expedition *see* haste
expeditious *see* fast
expert *see* proficient
explain
explicate *see* explain
expose *see* show
expunge *see* erase
exquisite
exterminate *see* annihilate
extinguish *see* annihilate
extol *see* praise
extraneous *see* irrelevant
extravagant *see* excessive
extreme *see* excessive
extricate

facile *see* easy
factor *see* element
fade *see* disappear
fair
fair *see* average, beautiful
faith *see* trust

faithful
famed *see* famous
familiar *see* common
famous
fascinate *see* charm
fast
fast *see* faithful
fat
fatal
fatigue *see* tire
fatuous *see* foolish
fault *see* blemish
faultless *see* perfect
faze *see* embarrass
fear
fearless *see* brave
fervor *see* passion
fetter *see* hobble
field
fight *see* oppose
figure
figure *see* calculate, form
fill *see* satisfy
filthy *see* dirty
final *see* last
fine *see* exquisite
finish *see* complete
fire *see* passion
fit *see* adapt
fix *see* predicament
flabbergast *see* surprise
flash
flash *see* moment
flat *see* level
flaunt *see* show
flaw *see* blemish
flawless *see* perfect
fleet *see* fast
flexible
flimsy *see* fragile
fling *see* throw
flood *see* flow
flow
flow *see* stem
flush *see* level
follow
foolish
forbid
force
force *see* strength
foremost *see* chief
forestall *see* prevent

foretell
forget *see antonym at*
    remember
forgive
form
forthright *see* frank
forward *see* send
foul *see* contaminate
foundation *see* base
fracas *see* brawl
fracture *see* break
fragile
frangible *see* fragile
frank
fray *see* brawl
free-for-all *see* brawl
freehanded *see* liberal
fresh *see* new
fret *see* brood
fright *see* fear
frighten
frigid *see* cold
fritter *see* waste
frosty *see* cold
frugal *see* sparing
fruitless *see* futile
fulfill *see* satisfy
furious *see* angry
furtive *see* secret
fury *see* anger
fuse *see* mix
futile

gad *see* wander
gag *see* joke
gallivant *see* wander
gape *see* gaze
gargantuan *see* enormous
garner *see* reap
gather
gather *see* reap
gaunt *see* lean
gawk *see* gaze
gaze
gear *see* equipment
gelid *see* cold
generous *see* liberal
genesis *see* beginning
genuine *see* authentic
ghastly
gigantic *see* enormous
glacial *see* cold

glad
glare *see* gaze
gleam *see* flash
glean *see* reap
glide *see* slide
glimmer *see* flash
glint *see* flash
glisten *see* flash
glitter *see* flash
goal *see* intention
grand
grasp *see* understand
great *see* large
grieve
grim *see* ghastly
grimy *see* dirty
grisly *see* ghastly
gross *see* whole
ground *see* base
groundless *see* baseless
groundwork *see* base
grubby *see* dirty
gruesome *see* ghastly
gruff
guard *see* defend
guide
guileless *see* naive
gusto *see* zest
gyrate *see* turn

habit
hale *see* healthy
halt *see* stop
handcuff *see* hobble
handsome *see* beautiful
handy *see* dexterous
haphazard *see* chance
happen
happening *see* occurrence
happy *see* glad
harass
harmonize *see* correspond
harry *see* harass
harvest *see* reap
haste
hasty *see* impetuous
hateful
hazard *see* endanger
headlong *see* impetuous
headstrong *see* obstinate
healthy
heap

heavy
heedful *see* careful
heedless *see* careless
hefty *see* heavy
heritage
hero *see* celebrity
hide
hide *see* block
hint *see* suggest
hobble
hogtie *see* hobble
hold *see* contain
holler *see* yell
hollow *see* vain
hoodwink *see* deceive
hope *see* expect
horror *see* fear
hostility *see* enmity
hot *see antonym at* cold
hound *see* harass
howl *see* yell
hubbub *see* noise
huge *see* enormous
hullabaloo *see* noise
humdrum *see* dull
hurl *see* throw
hurry *see* haste

icy *see* cold
idea
ideal
idle *see* baseless, inactive,
 vain
idolize *see* revere
illustration *see* example
illustrious *see* famous
imbue
imitate
immaterial *see* irrelevant
immature *see* young
immense *see* enormous
immoderate *see* excessive
impartial *see* fair
impeccable *see* perfect
imperative *see* urgent
imperfection *see* blemish
imperil *see* endanger
impertinent *see* irrelevant
impetuous
imply *see* suggest
import *see* importance
importance

imposing *see* grand
impute *see* attribute
inactive
inadvertent *see* careless
inaugurate *see* begin
incandescent *see* bright
inception *see* origin
incessant *see* continual
incident *see* occurrence
incite *see* provoke
include
increase
indefatigable *see* tireless
indicate
indifferent *see* average
indignant *see* angry
indignation *see* anger
indispensable
industrious *see* diligent
industry *see* business
ineffectual *see* futile
inelastic *see* stiff
inert *see* inactive
infantile *see* young
inflexible *see* stiff
information *see* knowledge
infraction *see* breach
infringement *see* breach
ingenuous *see* naive
ingest *see* eat
ingredient *see* element
inheritance *see* heritage
inhibit *see* restrain
initiate *see* begin
inordinate *see* excessive
inquire *see* ask
inquiry
inquisition *see* inquiry
insinuate *see* suggest
instance *see* example
instant *see* moment
instruct *see* teach
insufficient *see antonym at*
 sufficient
insulate *see* isolate
insult *see* offend
intellectual *see* intelligent
intelligent
intemperate *see* excessive
intent *see* intention
intention
interim *see* temporary

intermission *see* pause
interpret *see* explain
interrogate *see* ask
intimate *see* suggest
intractable *see* obstinate
intrepid *see* brave
intricate *see* complex
intuition *see* reason
invert *see* reverse
investigation *see* inquiry
involved *see* complex
irate *see* angry
ire *see* anger
ireful *see* angry
irk *see* annoy
irksome *see* boring
irrelevant
irritate *see* annoy
isolate
issue *see* stem

jam *see* predicament
jeopardize *see* endanger
jiffy *see* moment
job *see* task
join
joke
joyful *see* glad
joyous *see* glad
judgment *see* reason
just *see* fair
jut *see* bulge
juvenile *see* young

keen *see* cry
keep
keep *see* observe
keeping *see* care
knowledge

labor *see* work
lackluster *see* dull
laconic
laggard *see* slow
lambent *see* bright
lament *see* grieve
languor *see* lethargy
lank *see* lean
lanky *see* lean
large
large *see antonym at* small
lassitude *see* lethargy

last
late *see* tardy
latent *see* inactive
laud *see* praise
launch *see* begin
lax *see* negligent
lead *see* guide
leading *see* chief
lean
learning *see* knowledge
legacy *see* heritage
leisurely *see* slow
lengthen *see antonym at*
  shorten
leniency *see* mercy
lessen *see* decrease
lethal *see* fatal
lethargy
level
level *see* aim
liberal
lighten *see* relieve
lighthearted *see* glad
link *see* join
little *see* small
lively *see* active, *see antonym*
  at dull
loathsome *see* offensive
lonely *see* alone
lonesome *see* alone
lore *see* knowledge
lovely *see* beautiful
loyal *see* faithful
ludicrous *see* foolish
luminary *see* celebrity
luminous *see* bright
luscious *see* delicious
lustrous *see* bright
lying *see* dishonest

macabre *see* ghastly
mad *see* angry
magnificent *see* grand
main *see* chief
majestic *see* grand
mammoth *see* enormous
manacle *see* hobble
manifest *see* apparent
mannerism *see* affectation
margin *see* border
marked *see* noticeable
mash *see* crush

massive *see* heavy
matter *see* subject
meander *see* wander
mediocre *see* average
medium *see* average
meet *see* satisfy
melancholy *see* sad
melee *see* brawl
mendacious *see* dishonest
mercy
merge *see* mix
merit *see* earn
mettlesome *see* brave
middling *see* average
might *see* strength
millstone *see* burden
mimic *see* imitate
mindful *see* careful
mingle *see* mix
miniature *see* small
minuscule *see* small
minute *see* moment
minute *see* small
mislead *see* deceive
mitigate *see* relieve
mix
mock *see* ridicule
model *see* ideal
mollify *see* pacify
moment
moneyed *see* rich
monotonous *see* boring
mope *see* brood
moral
mortal *see* fatal
motif *see* figure
mound *see* heap
mount *see* rise
mourn *see* grieve
move
moving
mulish *see* obstinate
multiply *see* increase
munificent *see* liberal
murky *see* dark
muscular
mysterious
mystify *see* perplex

naive
name *see* celebrity
narrate *see* describe

nascence *see* beginning
nasty *see* offensive
natural *see* naive
nature *see* disposition
necessary *see* indispensable
neglectful *see* negligent
negligent
new
nimble *see* dexterous
nitpick *see* quibble
noise
notable *see* celebrity, famous
note *see* see
noted *see* famous
notice *see* see
noticeable
notion *see* idea
novel *see* new

obese *see* fat
object *see* intention
objective *see* fair, intention
obligate *see* force
oblige *see* force
obliterate *see* annihilate
obscure *see antonym at*
  famous
obscure *see* block
observe
observe *see* see
obstinate
obstruct *see* block
obviate *see* prevent
obvious *see* apparent
occasion *see* opportunity
occult *see* mysterious
occur *see* happen
occurrence
odd *see* strange
odious *see* hateful, offensive
odor *see* smell
offend
offensive
offensive *see* hateful
old
open *see* frank
openhanded *see* liberal
opening *see* opportunity
opportunity
oppose
option *see* choice
orbit *see* range

ordinary *see* common
origin
original *see* new
originate *see* stem
oscillate *see* swing
otiose *see* vain
outcome *see* effect
outdo *see* excel
outfit *see* equipment
outlandish *see* strange
outline
outrage *see* offend
outspoken *see* frank
outstrip *see* excel
overdue *see* tardy
overweight *see* fat
own *see* acknowledge

pacify
pact *see* agreement
palliate *see* relieve
pandemonium *see* noise
panic *see* fear, frighten
parade *see* show
paraphernalia *see* equip-
    ment
pardon *see* forgive
parody *see* imitate
part *see* separate
partial *see antonym at* whole
partner
passion
patent *see* apparent
pattern *see* figure, ideal
pause
peaceful *see* calm
peak *see* summit
peculiar *see* strange
pedestrian *see* dull
peer *see* gaze
peeve *see* annoy
perceive *see* see
perennial *see* continual
perfect
perform
permanent *see antonym at*
    temporary
permeate *see* imbue
permit *see antonym at* forbid
perpetual *see* continual
perplex
personage *see* celebrity

personality *see* disposition
pervade *see* imbue
pester *see* harass
petite *see* small
philanthropic *see* benevolent
pickle *see* predicament
pigheaded *see* obstinate
pile *see* heap
pilot *see* guide
pinnacle *see* summit
pitch *see* throw
pity
placate *see* pacify
placid *see* calm
plague *see* harass
plain *see* apparent
plane *see* level
plenteous *see* plentiful
plentiful
plight *see* predicament
plucky *see* brave
plump *see* fat
poignant *see* moving
point *see* aim
pointless *see* futile
poison *see* contaminate
pollute *see* contaminate
ponderous *see* heavy
poor *see antonym at* rich
portly *see* fat
pose *see* affectation
power *see* strength
practice *see* habit
praise
precipitate *see* impetuous
preclude *see* prevent
predicament
preeminent *see* famous
preference *see* choice
preposterous *see* foolish
preserve *see* defend
pressing *see* urgent
pretty *see* beautiful
prevent
primary *see* chief
prime *see* chief
principal *see* chief
prize *see* appreciate
probe *see* inquiry
proceed *see* stem
produce
proficient

profile *see* form, outline
prohibit *see* forbid
project *see* bulge
prominent *see* noticeable
prompt *see antonym at* tardy
propel *see* push
property *see* quality
prophesy *see* foretell
propitiate *see* pacify
proscribe *see* forbid
protect *see* defend
protrude *see* bulge
province *see* field
provisional *see* temporary
provoke
provoke *see* annoy
pudgy *see* fat
puerile *see* young
pugnacious *see* belligerent
pull *see antonym at* push
purpose *see* intention
purview *see* range
push
puzzle *see* perplex

quake *see* shake
quality
quandary *see* predicament
quarrel *see* argue
query *see* ask
question *see* ask
quibble
quick *see* fast
quiescent *see* inactive
quip *see* joke
quit *see* stop
quiver *see* shake
quiz *see* ask

racket *see* noise
radiant *see* bright
rage *see* anger
rail *see* scold
ramble *see* wander
random *see* chance
range
range *see* wander
rapid *see* fast
rate *see* earn
ration *see* distribute
raze *see* destroy
reach *see* range

real
real *see* authentic
realm *see* field
reap
reason
reason *see* think
rebuff *see* refuse
rebuke *see* admonish
recalcitrant *see* obstinate
recall *see* remember
recede
recess *see* pause
recite *see* describe
reckon *see* calculate
reclaim *see* save
recollect *see* remember
recount *see* describe
rectify *see* correct
redeem *see* save
redress *see* correct
reduce *see* decrease
refer *see* attribute
reflect *see* think
refuge *see* shelter
refuse
regale *see* amuse
reject *see* refuse
rejoice *see antonym at* grieve
relate *see* describe
relent *see* yield
relevant *see antonym at*
   irrelevant
reliance *see* trust
relieve
relish *see* zest
remark *see* see
remedy *see* correct
remember
remiss *see* negligent
renowned *see* famous
repel *see antonym at* charm
repellent *see* hateful
reply *see* answer
report *see* describe
reprimand *see* admonish
reproach *see* admonish
reprove *see* admonish
repulsive *see* offensive
requisite *see* indispensable
rescue *see* save
resentment *see* anger
reserve *see* keep

resilient *see* flexible
resist *see* oppose
resolve *see* decide
respite *see* pause
respond *see* answer
restrain
result *see* effect, follow
retain *see* keep
reticent *see* laconic
retort *see* answer
retract *see* recede
retreat *see* recede, shelter
revere
reverse
revile *see* scold
revise *see* correct
revolting *see* offensive
revolve *see* turn
rich
ridicule
ridiculous *see* foolish
righteous *see* moral
rigid *see* stiff
rile *see* annoy
rim *see* border
rise
rise *see* beginning, stem
risk *see* endanger
roam *see* wander
roar *see* yell
robust *see* healthy
rock *see* agitate, swing
root *see* origin
rotate *see* turn
rotund *see* fat
rouse *see* provoke
rout *see* defeat
route *see* send
rove *see* wander
ruin *see* destroy
rule *see* decide
rush *see* flow

sad
safeguard *see* defend
salient *see* noticeable
sanctuary *see* shelter
satisfactory *see* sufficient
satisfy
saturate *see* imbue
save
save *see antomym at* waste

scant *see antonym at* plentiful
scare *see* frighten
scent *see* smell
scholarship *see* knowledge
school *see* teach
scintillate *see* flash
scold
scope *see* range
scorch *see* burn
scrap *see* brawl
scrape *see* brawl
scrawny *see* lean
screen *see* block
scrumptious *see* delicious
scuffle *see* brawl
sear *see* burn
seclude *see* isolate
second *see* moment
secret
secrete *see* hide
sedulous *see* diligent
see
seethe *see* boil
segregate *see* isolate
selection *see* choice
send
sensible *see* aware
separate
sequester *see* isolate
serene *see* calm
settle *see* decide
sever *see* separate
severe
shackle *see* hobble
shadowy *see* dark
shady *see* dark
shake
shake *see* agitate
shape *see* form
shatter *see* break
shelter
shepherd *see* guide
shield *see* defend
ship *see* send
shiver *see* shake
shorten
shout *see* yell
shove *see* push
show
shroud *see* block
shudder *see* shake
significance *see* importance

silhouette *see* outline
silly *see* foolish
simmer *see* boil
simple *see* easy, naive
simulate *see* imitate
simultaneous *see* contemporary
sinewy *see* muscular
singe *see* burn
singular *see* strange
skepticism *see* uncertainty
skid *see* slide
skilled *see* proficient
skillful *see* proficient
skinny *see* lean
slack *see* negligent
slide
slip *see* slide
slipshod *see* sloppy
sloppy
slovenly *see* sloppy
slow
small
small *see antonym at* large
smart *see* intelligent
smash *see* break, crush
smell
smooth *see* level
snare *see* catch
snug *see* comfortable
soar *see* rise
sob *see* cry
solemnize *see* observe
solicitous *see* thoughtful
solitary *see* alone
sorrow *see* grieve
sorrowful *see* sad
sound *see* healthy
sour
source *see* origin
sparing
sparkle *see* flash
speak
specimen *see* example
speed *see* haste
speedy *see* fast
sphere *see* field
spin *see* turn
splinter *see* break
spring *see* stem
spurn *see* refuse
squabble *see* argue

squalid *see* dirty
squander *see* waste
squash *see* crush
stack *see* heap
standard *see* ideal
stare *see* gaze
start *see antonym at* stop
start *see* begin
startle *see* frighten
stately *see* grand
staunch *see* faithful
steadfast *see* faithful
stealthy *see* secret
steer *see* guide
stem
stern *see* severe
stew *see* boil
stiff
stimulate *see* provoke
stingy *see antonym at* liberal
stir *see* provoke
stirring *see* moving
stodgy *see* dull
stop
storm *see* attack
stout *see* fat
straightforward *see* frank
strange
stray *see* swerve, wander
stream *see* flow
strength
strict *see* severe
strident *see* vociferous
strife *see* conflict
striking *see* noticeable
stubborn *see* obstinate
subject
submit *see* yield
subscribe *see* assent
subside *see* decrease
substantiate *see* confirm
succeed *see* follow
succumb *see* yield
sufficient
suffuse *see* imbue
suggest
summit
sunder *see* separate
supervision *see* care
supple *see* flexible
surpass *see* excel
surprise

surreptitious *see* secret
survey *see* see
suspension *see* pause
sway *see* swing
sweep *see* range
swerve
swift *see* fast
swing
swirl *see* turn
sympathy *see* pity
synchronous *see* contemporary

taciturn *see* laconic
taint *see* contaminate
talk *see* speak
tangled *see* complex
tardy
tart *see* sour
task
taunt *see* ridicule
teach
tedious *see* boring
temperament *see* disposition
temporary
tendency
tenor *see* tendency
tense *see* stiff
terminal *see* last
terminate *see* complete
terrify *see* frighten
territory *see* field
terror *see* fear
terrorize *see* frighten
theme *see* subject
think
thought *see* idea
thoughtful
thoughtless *see* careless
thrifty *see* sparing
throw
thrust *see* push
tide *see* flow
tightlipped *see* laconic
tiny *see* small
tire
tireless
tiresome *see* boring
toil *see* work
tolerable *see* average
toothsome *see* delicious
topic *see* subject

torpor *see* lethargy
toss *see* throw
total *see* whole
touch *see* move
touching *see* moving
trade *see* business
tradition *see* heritage
traffic *see* business
train *see* aim, teach
trait *see* quality
tranquil *see* calm
transgression *see* breach
transmit *see* send
transpose *see* reverse
trap *see* catch
travail *see* work
treasure *see* appreciate
tremble *see* shake
tremendous *see* enormous
trend *see* tendency
trepidation *see* fear
trespass *see* breach
trial *see* burden
tribulation *see* burden
true *see* authentic, faithful, real
truncate *see* shorten
trust
trust *see* care
turf *see* field
turn
twinkle *see* flash
twist *see* distort

ultimate *see* last
unaffected *see* naive
unavailing *see* futile
unbiased *see* fair
uncertainty
undaunted *see* brave
underhand *see* secret
understand
understanding *see* reason
unflagging *see* tireless
unfounded *see* baseless
uninspired *see* dull
unite *see* join
unkempt *see* sloppy

unlikeness *see* difference
unprejudiced *see* fair
unquestionable *see* authentic
unsophisticated *see* naive
untangle *see* extricate
untiring *see* tireless
untruthful *see* dishonest
unwarranted *see* baseless
unwearied *see* tireless
upbraid *see* scold
uproar *see* noise
upshot *see* effect
urgent
useful *see antonym at* futile
useless *see* futile
usher *see* guide

vacant *see* empty
vacuous *see* empty
vague *see* ambiguous
vain
vain *see* futile
valiant *see* brave
validate *see* confirm
valorous *see* brave
value *see* appreciate
vanish *see* disappear
vanquish *see* defeat
variation *see* difference
vast *see* enormous
vaunt *see* boast
veer *see* swerve
venerate *see* revere
venturesome *see* adventurous
verge *see* border
verify *see* confirm
vex *see* annoy
vibrate *see* swing
view *see* see
vigilant *see* careful
vigorous *see* active
vile *see* offensive
violation *see* breach
virtuous *see* moral
vituperate *see* scold
vociferous

void *see* empty

wail *see* cry
wander
want *see* desire
warp *see* distort
waste
watchful *see* careful
waver *see* swing
wealthy *see* rich
weariless *see* tireless
weary *see* tire
wee *see* small
weep *see* cry
weight *see* importance
weighty *see* heavy
well *see* healthy
whirl *see* turn
whole
wholesome *see* healthy
whoop *see* yell
win *see* earn
wisecrack *see* joke
wish *see* desire
withhold *see* keep
witticism *see* joke
woebegone *see* sad
wont *see* habit
work
worry *see* brood
worship *see* revere
wrangle *see* argue
wrath *see* anger
wrathful *see* angry
wreck *see* destroy

yell
yield
yield *see* produce
young
youthful *see* young
yummy *see* delicious

zeal *see* passion
zenith *see* summit
zest